THE PSYCHOLOGY OF STRESS

Why do I get stressed? How can I manage my stress symptoms? How do neurodiversity, culture, and individual experiences affect stress responses?

The Psychology of Stress combines knowledge from neuroscience and the psychological and physiological underpinnings of stress to offer a scientific approach to understanding and managing symptoms. It provides practical and accessible interventions to help overcome the effects of dealing with overwhelming experiences and also brings in the role of family and community in helping to live a more stress-free life.

Using a framework that integrates physical and mental health, *The Psychology of Stress* provides an overview of the key aspects of stress and coping, and reveals how to integrate scientific, therapeutic and movement-based approaches to deal with stress and enhance wellbeing.

Charlotte Mottram who has completed her BSc in Psychology and Health is a psychology teacher for A-Levels. She is also certified Pilates instructor and a member of the Charted Institute for the Management of Sport and Physical Activity (CIMSPA). She is very passionate about bringing her two favourite topics psychology and movement. Her Pilates classes are filled with energy and snippets about how this affects the mind and the body. Charlotte is also a core-member and supporter of Trauma Informed Practice Services (TIPS).

Alison Woodward is a Certified Transactional Analyst (CTA), Clinical Supervisor and UKCP registered Psychotherapist and works both in Private Practice and at Bournemouth University as a Senior Lecturer in the Psychology Department and is a Teaching Fellow of the Higher Education Academy. She has previously been joint Clinical Lead at the Sexual Trauma and Recovery Service (STARS) in Dorset and her extensive clinical experience and research interests are in working with the symptoms Complex PTSD and supporting people who have experienced early childhood trauma understand what has happened to them through a trauma-informed lens, shifting belief from 'this is about me' to 'this is about what has happened to me'. Alison is passionate about breaking down the barriers to a trauma-informed approach and delivers many training courses for organisations to support accessible education about the impact of trauma on all of us. Alison is a Co-Director of the UK Charity, Trauma Informed Practice Services (TIPS).

Shanti Farrington is a Chartered Psychologist and works as an Associate Psychologist with the NHS, UK and a Counsellor (MBACP, UK). Having completed her PhD from Bangor University, she is an Academic Neuropsychologist and a Principal Academic in Psychology at Bournemouth University. She is also has been associated with MRC Cognition and Brain Sciences Unit, University of Cambridge, as a visiting researcher and a Fellow of the Higher Education Academy. Her areas of active research focus on stroke, brain injury and complex trauma. She is passionate about integrating research into rehabilitation and counselling. She has taught psychology in several UK Universities and in India. Shanti is a Co-Director of the UK Charity, Trauma Informed Practice Services (TIPS, a CIC). She is currently working towards her Doctorate in Counselling Psychology in UK.

THE PSYCHOLOGY OF EVERYTHING

People are fascinated by psychology, and what makes humans tick. Why do we think and behave the way we do? We've all met armchair psychologists claiming to have the answers, and people that ask if psychologists can tell what they're thinking. The Psychology of Everything is a series of books which debunk the popular myths and pseudo-science surrounding some of life's biggest questions.

The series explores the hidden psychological factors that drive us, from our subconscious desires and aversions to our natural social instincts. Absorbing, informative, and always intriguing, each book is written by an expert in the field, examining how research-based knowledge compares with popular wisdom, and showing how psychology can truly enrich our understanding of modern life.

Applying a psychological lens to an array of topics and contemporary concerns – from sex, to fashion, to conspiracy theories – The Psychology of Everything will make you look at everything in a new way.

Titles in the series:

For more information about this series, please visit: www.routledgetextbooks.com/textbooks/thepsychologyofeverything/

THE PSYCHOLOGY OF STRESS

CHARLOTTE MOTTRAM, ALISON WOODWARD
AND SHANTI FARRINGTON

Routledge
Taylor & Francis Group

LONDON AND NEW YORK

First published 2026
by Routledge
4 Park Square, Milton Park, Abingdon, Oxon OX14 4RN

and by Routledge
605 Third Avenue, New York, NY 10158

Routledge is an imprint of the Taylor & Francis Group, an informa business

British Library Cataloguing-in-Publication Data
A catalogue record for this book is available from the British Library

ISBN: 9781032883731 (hbk)
ISBN: 9781032869759 (pbk)
ISBN: 9781003537410 (ebk)

DOI: 10.4324/9781003537410

Typeset in Joanna
by Newgen Publishing UK

Dedication

We would like to thank our clients who always teach us and allow us to learn with them in the process of their journey. We would like to acknowledge their trust in us and their courage to grow in their journey of life.

CONTENTS

OVERVIEW

Stress is a word that most of us are familiar with, and use it in our daily life. We are aware that as stress builds up over time, it can lead to several mental and physical health issues. Stress is part of our lives and can usually be resolved relatively easily by individuals, depending on their resilience and ability to deal with the cause of the stress. A certain amount of stress is normally tolerated and is required to successfully perform, be motivated and carry on with daily life. However, life experiences like adverse childhood events, repeated daily hassles, fatigue and cognitive overload can start building more stress in a person, which can become unmanageable. Experiencing stress therefore can be good but the level of what "*good*" is depends on everyone's own experiences. Excess stress can result in affecting wellbeing from a social, physical, emotional perspective and sometimes leads to additional diagnosis such as chronic fatigue syndrome and other functional disorders. Understanding how our *ability* to manage stress depends on the body's systems, the resilience in that individual, and the available and accessible toolkits.

The Psychology of Stress book aims to consolidate the current understanding around stress. Specifically, by bringing together and linking the reasons of why stress can affect different aspects of individuals life and the scientific understanding of the reason why this is dependent on individual differences. Understanding the psychology of stress, will not only support individuals to be empowered to manage their stress symptoms effectively but also encourage them to engage with appropriate methods to overcome their stress and work on better managing their toolkits.

Bringing knowledge from neuroscience along with the psychological, physiological, and somatic underpinnings of stress we offer a more holistic, but scientifically integrated, approach to manage symptoms of stress. This book integrates academic and non-academic perspectives with everyday issues, debunking the myths and prejudices in dealing with stress. It aims to bring together tools, therapeutic inputs and physical and movement aspects that help alleviate stress and move away from only the mental perspective.

This book explores understanding the effect of not only mental health and everyday issues around stress, but brings in a more clinical, neurodiversity-based aspect, alongside consideration of cultural differences, to explain the way we respond to any stress. Providing more practical but accessible intervention to help overcome the effects of dealing with overwhelming experiences. This book aims to be a quick handbook for an easy read with skills that can easily be applied to anyone reading this. The book uses a framework that integrates practical, therapeutic, and neuroscientific approaches to work with evidence-based practise in in dealing with stress whilst also bringing in the role of family and community in facilitating and overcoming the milestones in living a more stress-free life.

As part of the 'Psychology of Everything' series, this book is written in a style that is easy to understand. It is aimed people who want to know more about what causes stress for each person, what do they do and how can they improve their coping styles. Professionals (e.g. holistic practitioners, yoga and Pilate instructors, occupational/physio therapists, clinicians, counsellors, psychologists, academics etc.) may find this as a one stop shop to bring together historical, theoretical, psychological, physiological, and other factors underlying stress and coping. Overall, this book offers a concise, and engaging review to empower readers to begin to ask questions about "Why do I get stressed?" and explore "What do I do? And how can I cope better?"

Your body loves to move…use that to help shift the focus of stress!

ACKNOWLEDGEMENT

The authors would like to thank Vanessa Oliveira Pessoa for taking the time to read our draft. Our families have always been patient in the process of writing and continue to love us, despite our obsession with work. Their continued support allows us to ensure we find a balance between our work and finding time to be with our loved ones, thereby reducing our own stress in the journey of life. Our families have been invaluable throughout the process, and we thank Ben, Imogen, Billy and Cody Mottram; Sam, Charlotte and Bethan Woodward; and Jon and Ragini Farrington for their patience and love.

PREFACE

Stress is key in everyone's life, but like salt, a necessary ingredient to taste and enjoy life, in excess it can be damaging. You perhaps have picked up this book because you may be feeling overwhelmed, or you have recently noticed that there's something off balance in your life… and you realise it may be stress and are looking for some help or advice.

This book provides a brief overview of stress to give you a better understanding of the possible emotional, physical, health and psychological effects and impacts. It is ideal for someone who wants to delve deeper into the psychology of stress and can help you also understand how sometimes getting out of your head or thoughts and into your body may help you cope, especially when you are feeling overwhelmed. It will also be useful for students and qualified practitioners who want to know more about the body-mind effect of stress and how to integrate scientific, therapeutic and movement-based approaches to bring a more practical and efficient way to deal with individual stressors. Some parts of this book may provide a quick overview of certain aspects of stress and coping, while other chapters expand on knowledge and bring together several aspects of stress and the tools to help manage it but from a more diverse and cultural perspective. Finally, a section addresses the common myths and assumptions one may have, with easy-to-follow tools or practices.

1

INTRODUCTION TO STRESS

The intention of this chapter is for the reader to understand the concepts of stress, how that experiencing it can be helpful, how it differs to anxiety, and how simultaneously it can also be the catalyst for mental health concerns and other disorders/issues. Initially outlining definitions of stress this chapter introduces the reader to a refreshing way to look at the impact that different life events, daily hassles and environments can have on our stress levels and responses. It defines some of the common terms used around stress, when people say "I'm really stressed" do they mean they are overloaded and experiencing stress, or just feeling something else? The chapter will explore whether all stress is bad and when is stress a beneficial experience, can stress be both good and bad? Finally, it sets out the framework for the rest of the book, and how staying curious about when is stress considered to be too much stress?

DEFINING STRESS AND HOW IT IMPACTS THE MIND AND BODY

What is stress? Stress is a universal part of the human condition, woven into the fabric of our daily lives. It is a response to external pressures or demands. These demands, or stressors, can arise from various external sources for example work deadlines, relationship conflicts, financial concerns, or significant life changes or from internal sources like our expectations and perceptions. Stress is an

DOI: 10.4324/9781003537410-1

appropriate reaction to tangible situations, typically tied to a specific event or set of circumstances and often diminishes once the stressor is resolved. It transcends cultures, ages, and circumstances, shaping our responses to life's demands and challenges, and is more than a fleeting sense of being overwhelmed, often triggered by external factors which are normally beyond one's own control. It is time-bound in nature, so when the stressor is removed or managed, there is usually a sense of relief. As we all might have noticed, stress can have a functional role – especially in small or moderate amounts it can have a purpose and helps with motivation.

The word "stress" is common in our modern language. We use it sometimes flippantly to describe a difficult situation or feeling which minimises the extent of the impact of feeling stressed. It is therefore important to recognise that stress is a complex experience which operates on a spectrum, ranging from fleeting moments of pressure that motivate action to chronic strains that erode our wellbeing over time. Whether it's a looming deadline, a disagreement with a loved one, or a significant life change, "stress" is the term we often use to describe how we feel. But what does it truly mean to be stressed? Stress can have biological, physical and emotional effects on individuals. On a biological level, stress is the body's adaptive response to perceived threats or demands. This response is not only seen in humans but has evolved from our evolutionary history and is also seen in animals. This response has been necessary to ensure our survival, such that when faced with danger from a predator (in ancient times), or an external trigger or a deadline (in the modern workplace) our body activates the well-known fight or flight response (for more details see Chapter 2).

Psychological perspective: Stress is a universal experience, although it is deeply subjective. Stress is deeply tied to how an individual perceives that situation or trigger. The way it manifests and affects individuals varies widely, influenced by personality traits, life experiences, and available resources. Therefore, it is not just what happens to us, but how we interpret and react to the event(s). Psychologists often describe stress as arising from a perceived imbalance between demands and resources. For example, a public speaking engagement might exhilarate one individual while paralysing another. The difference lies in their internal appraisals. A situation that energises and motivates one person might overwhelm and immobilise another. These individual differences are shaped by factors such as temperament, personal history, and coping mechanisms. While someone who has a resilient mindset might thrive under the pressure of a tight deadline, viewing it as a challenge, while another might find the same scenario paralysing and anxiety-inducing and may view it as a threat. Appraising it as "threatening" can lead to a negative experience or sense of failure. How one appraises these situations or triggers are shaped by factors like past experiences, coping mechanisms, and personality traits.

A person with a strong sense of self-efficacy (a belief in their ability to handle challenges) is more likely to experience stress as motivating rather than debilitating. Traits that can be displayed in different personality types may be a risk factor for stress. Defining our personality type by the typical characteristics that can be displayed can be helpful. For instance, someone who has a high drive, is more competitive may have a sense of urgency and control (for example someone with a more type A personality) may be more prone to stress and stress related illness. Similarly, someone with a trait of being a perfectionist may set unrealistically high standards for themselves, and when they are unable to meet those expectations, often may be faced with a sense of failure. Hence leading to chronic dissatisfaction and stress. While individuals with resilient traits often will look at adversity or roadblocks as a stepping stone or growth for opportunity and hence are normally better equipped to manage stress. This often can be noticed in people with type B personality who may be easier going and flexible. Compared to personality C type individuals who are known to be more passive in nature and often avoid conflicts. While someone with a personality D type is also known as "distressed" personality and may have a more anxious predisposition.

STRESS AS A DOUBLE-EDGED SWORD

Stress is commonly perceived as inherently negative, but sadly this view overlooks its dual nature. While stress can indeed be debilitating, contributing to burnout, anxiety, and physical illness, it can also serve as a powerful motivator that drives growth and achievement. Stress takes on its much darker role when it becomes overwhelming, a state known as *distress*, this harmful form of stress arises when the demands placed may exceed our ability to cope effectively. However the motivating aspect of stress is known as *eustress*, which invigorates and uplifts. Whilst distress is draining, leaving individuals feeling helpless, exhausted, or despairing, eustress is often desired to achieve – a true double-edged sword as it is difficult sometimes to find the balance between healthy and unhealthy levels of stress. When we experience too much distress in a repeated and long-lasting way stress can turn into *chronic distress*, which gradually erodes both our physical health and psychological resilience. Over time, it can lead to conditions such as heart disease, weakened immunity, and mental health disorders like depression and anxiety. Sometimes prolonged stress can also lead to someone developing a chronic fatigue disorder that could need significant changes to their lifestyle to manage and cope with their own expectations of achievement and stress levels.

Understanding stress and being more aware of our own triggers and limitations, allows individuals to harness stress in ways that enhance their lives. As described above positive stress can manifest as eustress. This occurs when challenges are seen as manageable and within our ability to overcome them, providing opportunities for personal growth. For example, preparing for a job interview, training for a marathon, or studying for an important exam all involve stress, yet they also come with a sense of purpose and accomplishment. This form of stress energises and motivates us to perform at our optimum capacity, while reinforcing the idea that not all stress is detrimental.

By recognising the dual nature of stress, we can better differentiate between the stress that propels us forward and the stress that holds us back. This awareness is a crucial step in managing our responses to life's challenges, allowing us to navigate them with greater resilience and balance. Stress is not just a biological or psychological response; it is a construct that is shaped by societal norms and expectations. Modern society often equates being busy with success, glorifying a relentless pace of life that leaves little room for rest. This cultural narrative normalises stress, framing it as an inevitable and even essential part of achievement, often also leaving individuals with feelings of guilt if and when they choose to slow down, to prioritise themselves. For example, in the workplace, employees who stay late or answer emails at all hours are often praised for their dedication, even if this behaviour comes at the cost of their wellbeing. Similarly, students are expected to juggle academic demands, extracurricular activities, and social lives, often at the expense of their mental health. Shifting this narrative requires redefining success to include balance and wellbeing. It also calls for systemic changes, such as promoting flexible work environments, prioritising mental health resources, and fostering cultures that value rest as much as productivity. To navigate the complexities of stress, it is essential to start with a comprehensive understanding of oneself and one's social, cultural and other environments so that we can develop strategies to harness its benefits while mitigating its harms.

HOW IS STRESS DIFFERENT FROM ANXIETY

What is anxiety? Anxiety is a feeling of fear, dread and/or uneasiness, which is a more internal state or trait of mind that may occur even in the absence of an identifiable stressor. It can be triggered by external factors, but often not tied to specific external events. Anxiety often involves an exaggerated response to perceived threats, with the mind anticipating worst-case scenarios to try to control and manage an outcome which is, in that moment, unknown. Usually with anxiety the worry is more internal and stems from one's own perceptions of life. It can be more chronic in nature and a more permanent state of mind in some individuals. Sometimes the intensity of anxiety experienced by the individual can often be disproportionate to the actual situation that is happening and therefore the response exceeds what the situation warrants. This can be incredibly distressing for individuals and sometimes causes symptoms that are debilitating to functioning well in everyday life. When we experience anxiety that is chronic, i.e. is experienced on more days than not over a distinct time-period, it may be helpful to get some support from medical or allied health professionals (general physicians, psychiatrists, psychologists or psychotherapists or counsellors).

Both stress and anxiety are emotional responses, and often there is a fine line between the two which can make it hard to distinguish between and may be quite intertwined. While distinct, they share a significant overlap in terms of how they are felt by individuals in the body and the impact that they have on our "usual" everyday functioning. It is helpful to remember when defining both, that stress is often caused by an external trigger, but anxiety can be defined as a more persistent state of internal worry which may not go away even if there are no external stressors. However, both stress and anxiety trigger similar physiological responses in the body. The activation of the sympathetic nervous system leads to an increase in heart rate, rapid breathing, and heightened alertness, which are common features of both states. This physiological overlap can make it difficult to discern whether someone is experiencing stress or anxiety, especially when stress becomes chronic and starts to mirror the symptoms typically associated with anxiety (explored further in Chapter 2).

Prolonged stress can sometimes act as a precursor to anxiety and the transition from stress to anxiety occurs subtly, without clear distinction, making it difficult to differentiate between the two. Chronic stress can heighten the brain's sensitivity to perceived threats, making individuals more susceptible to anxiety. For example, an employee who feels overburdened by work pressures might develop an ongoing fear of failure that extends beyond the workplace, which may be manifested as generalised anxiety. This shift may occur as the individual becomes hyper-aware of potential dangers, even in situations where there is no immediate threat.

This overlap between stress and anxiety can cause individuals to misinterpret their experiences, and in some cases, delay seeking appropriate help. Recognising this distinction will help reduce stigma. Many individuals dismiss anxiety as mere stress, overlooking its serious impact on mental health. Understanding the differences ensures that one can access timely targeted interventions. Often if you have developed anxiety, but are still interpreting it as a stress, using stress-focused approaches may often fail to address the deeper anxiety and internal perceptions of self. While if you are only addressing the anxiety and not recognising the stress, then anxiety focused treatments may not resolve the external stressors. Educating people about these differences empowers them to seek timely and tailored support, fostering healthier coping and overall well-being.

COGNITIVE PATTERNS AND STRESS

Cognitive patterns also play a key role in the connection between stress and anxiety. When stress leads to rumination (i.e. repeatedly thinking about a problem or situation) it can set the stage for anxiety to develop. The stress driven repetitive thinking fosters a sense of helplessness and a feeling that something catastrophic may occur. For instance, someone experiencing financial stress may become consumed with worry about the future, imagining worst-case scenarios that may never come to pass. This type of thinking can fuel anxiety, amplifying the stress that initially triggered the worry. To better illustrate the difference between stress and anxiety, consider the scenario of preparing for a public speaking engagement. One individual may feel nervous but focused, using the pressure of the upcoming presentation to enhance their performance. Once the presentation is over, their stress dissipates. In contrast, another person, despite thorough preparation, continues to worry excessively about being judged or failing. Even after the event has ended, they fixate on perceived mistakes, leading to ongoing distress. This distinction highlights the way anxiety can persist long after the stressor has passed, whereas stress tends to subside once the external pressure is removed.

Understanding the differences between stress and anxiety is crucial in determining the most effective approach to managing them. While the cognitive patterns of stress and anxiety are often enmeshed, understanding their differences is key to implementing the most effective strategies. In stress management, the goal is to address the external causes and develop coping mechanisms to handle them. Time management, relaxation techniques such as deep breathing, yoga, Pilates or progressive muscle relaxation, and problem-solving strategies are all effective ways to mitigate the impact of stress. We will look at how these can be used throughout this book. Anxiety management, however, often requires a focus on internal emotional and cognitive regulation. Cognitive Behavioural Therapy (CBT) is a highly effective treatment, helping individuals reframe irrational thoughts and replace them with a more balanced, constructive perspective. Mindfulness and meditation practices can foster present-moment awareness, reducing the tendency to ruminate. Gradual exposure therapy, where individuals confront feared situations in a controlled manner, can help desensitise them to anxiety-inducing scenarios.

STRESS AS AN EVOLUTIONARY MECHANISM

We have learnt already that stress exists on a spectrum ranging from the invigorating to the overwhelming. The American Psychological

Association (APA, 2015) defines stress as "*a normal reaction to everyday pressures*" and goes on to suggest that "*it can become unhealthy when it upsets day-to-day functioning*". It also reminds us that stress can involve changes to nearly every system of the body, which of course influences how individuals feel and behave when under stress.

This response has deep evolutionary roots. In prehistoric times, stress equipped humans to survive immediate threats, such as predators or environmental dangers, by triggering the fight or flight response. This physiological reaction involves the rapid release of stress hormones like adrenaline and cortisol, which prepare the body to act. While this mechanism was vital for survival in a hunter gatherer context, it has not adapted to modern stressors. Today, stress often arises from non-life-threatening sources, work deadlines, social conflicts, or financial worries yet our bodies react as though we are facing immediate physical danger. The mismatch between our evolutionary programming and modern life is a significant factor in the rise of chronic stress-related illnesses.

IS STRESS A GOOD OR A BAD THING?

As we introduced earlier in this chapter stress often has two faces or facets, **eustress** or **distress**, representing its potential for either benefit or harm. Eustress enhances performance by keeping individuals alert and engaged and is often associated with the Yerkes-Dodson Law (Yerkes & Dodson 1908, see Figure 1.1). This suggests that performance improves with increased stress—up to an optimal point. Often represented by the bell curve, the performance peaks at the midpoint of the curve and then the performance decreases. Therefore, as stress goes beyond this threshold, it can become counterproductive. For example, preparing for an exam might push a student to study diligently, but excessive worry could impair concentration and recall which could lead to experiencing anxiety symptoms. Therefore, the key to eustress is perception. When individuals view a challenge as an opportunity for growth, rather than a threat, they are more likely

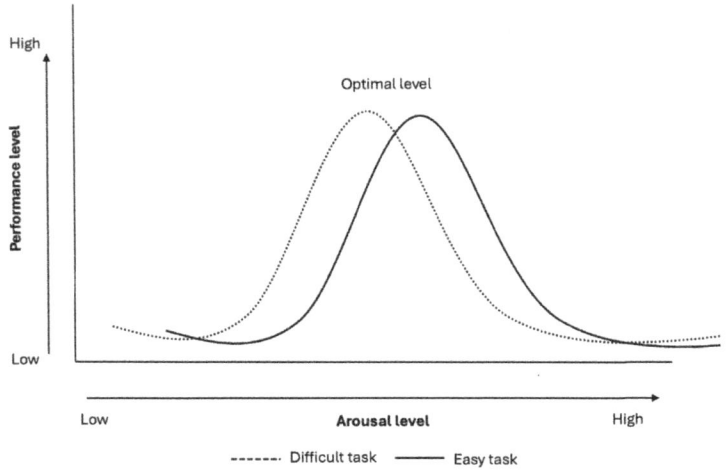

FIGURE 1.1 The Yerkes-Dodson Law of Arousal and Performance.

Source: Adapted from Yerkes-Dadson (1908).

to experience eustress. This positive framing fosters resilience and helps individuals navigate life's demands with confidence.

Stress becomes more distressing when the triggers are perceived as overwhelming and unmanageable. Often then contributing to feelings of anxiety, frustration, or helplessness. This can have far-reaching consequences for both mental and physical health. This shift often depends on individual factors including one's resilience, the capacity to tolerate change or adjustment and other environmental factors. Common examples of experiencing distress are when individuals experience burnout to excessive workloads or having a highly negative environment over time. Regular financial pressures, health challenges, having to care long-term for a loved one, having a toxic relationship with your significant other, having unresolved family issues and not having a secure base at home can also lead to developing long term stress responses.

Prolonged stress, when experienced as distress, may trigger the body's stress response repeatedly, and over time there may be a chronic activation of the hypothalamic-pituitary-adrenal (HPA) axis (expanded in Chapter 2). Over time, this can manifest by experiencing some physical health issues like hypertension (blood pressure), fatigue or developing back or shoulder pain etc. and then, if not stopped, developing into more long-term effects including weakening of the immune system or developing conditions like chronic fatigue syndrome, fibromyalgia, or acute stress disorder. Sometimes, the physical symptoms may also be coupled with changes in cognition which may manifest as difficulty in concentrating, unable to multitask, difficulty in making decisions, or forgetfulness.

When an individual experiences both physical and cognitive changes over a significant period it can become difficult to notice the original and repeated stress or triggers, therefore making the effects seem disproportionate or irrelevant. For example, someone who has been living with chronic stress from a high-pressured job role may not recognise the daily repeated impact of tight deadlines, new work coming in but instead might notice an extreme emotional reaction to forgetting to send a birthday card or missing a social function or a usual family event. In addition, long-term exposure to stress at a high level could also eventually lead to long lasting mental health problems such as developing mood changes including depression or anxiety or both and then also having emotional exhaustion – which may lead to suppressing or avoiding stressful situations and affect one's quality of life.

One of the most dangerous aspects of distress is its tendency to create a self-perpetuating cycle. For example, financial stress might lead to sleepless nights, which impair productivity, further worsening financial difficulties. This can often then lead to other issues and prevent the individual from resolving the crises and leads to more stress which can impact social and emotional aspects. To break this cycle, one must be aware of and notice the triggers to recognise whether they may need additional support from experts to help break this cycle. Perception is another critical factor in determining how stress is experienced.

Control or the lack of it, also plays a pivotal role in stress perception. Stress is more likely to become distress when people feel helpless or unable to influence a situation. Conversely, a sense of autonomy, even in small measures, can significantly mitigate the negative effects of stress. Feeling empowered to make decisions or enact change transforms the experience of stress, making it more manageable and less overwhelming. The context in which stress occurs adds another layer of complexity. External factors, including cultural norms, social expectations, and environmental conditions, shape how stress is experienced and expressed. In collectivist cultures, stress may arise from meeting familial or community obligations, while in individualist cultures, personal achievement and independence are often primary stressors.

Social pressures also contribute to how stress is perceived and managed. Modern society often glorifies being busy and overachievement, creating a "hustle culture" that equates constant productivity with success. This relentless push to do more can exacerbate stress, leading individuals to take on unsustainable workloads. Environmental conditions further influence stress levels. Urban environments with constant noise, congestion, and limited access to nature can heighten stress, whilst serene settings, such as parks or natural landscapes, have been shown to reduce it significantly. The presence or absence of supportive surroundings can profoundly impact how individuals experience and cope with stress.

This chapter focused on understanding stress as both a challenge and an opportunity. The remainder of the book will continue to explore the complexities of stress, providing both theoretical insights and practical strategies. Chapter 2 will delve into the biology of stress, examining the physiological processes behind stress responses and how different coping mechanisms impact these biological systems.

In Chapter 3, will broaden the lens by incorporating neurodiverse, cultural, and ethnic perspectives, offering a diverse range of views on how stress is experienced. Chapter 4 will focus on the powerful role of movement in managing stress, highlighting how physical activity, Pilates, yoga, and mindfulness practices contribute to stress reduction. Chapter 5 will challenge common misconceptions about stress, whilst separating fact from fiction to provide clearer insights. Finally, Chapter 6, road less travelled, will explore alternative and unconventional approaches to stress management, encouraging readers to explore new and lesser-known paths to resilience and well-being.

2

UNDERSTANDING THE BIOLOGY OF STRESS AND COPING MECHANISMS

The second chapter highlights the impact of stress on the body and how it can lead to physical and mental health issues. One needs to recognise when stress occurs and how it affects the individual physically and/or in their body, to help understand the benefit behind managing it, to eventually reduce the impact of stress. This chapter paints the picture of how our physical, psychological, and emotional responses shift and change. Finally, it brings in evidence from the basis of biology to not only understand our responses but also how we cope.

WHAT DO WE MEAN BY THE BODY'S RESPONSE TO STRESS?

Stress is deeply ingrained in the human experience, which has an impact on our body and mind. While it is natural for stress to arise in response to challenges, the way we manage and understand it can significantly influence our overall health and wellbeing. Stress is an innate survival mechanism designed to protect us from harm, it is

DOI: 10.4324/9781003537410-2

the product of millions of years of evolution. The "fight or flight" response, first described by Walter Cannon in the 1914 (Cannon, 1914), prepares the body to either confront a threat or escape from it. Its origin, initially stemmed from evolution, where our ancestors dealt with immediate physical dangers, like a predator in the wild. This threat today has shifted from physical dangers or basic survival to psychological dangers or stress factors, such as a work deadlines, financial worries, or conflicts within our relationships. Despite the difference in modern day threats, the body responds in fundamentally the same way, setting off a series of physiological reactions. The difficulty with this comes as the modern stressors do not resolve quickly. In the past when the threat was from a predator, we would have either fought, run or frozen and then recovered immediately. Instead, the modern stress factor is present for longer periods of time and our body therefore is continually producing stress hormones via the physiological reactions. It is this continued response that impacts the functioning of our bodies and is described in more detail below.

This physiological reaction to any stress often begins in the brain, specifically within the hypothalamus, which often activates the hypothalamic pituitary adrenal gland (which also functions as the body's stress command centre) to release hormones like cortisol and adrenaline to help the body activate and respond. These hormones prepare the body and respond effectively. The hypothalamus releases corticotropin releasing hormone (CRH), prompting the pituitary gland to secrete adrenocorticotropic hormone (ACTH). ACTH travels through the bloodstream to the adrenal glands, triggering the release of adrenaline and cortisol.

These stress hormones produce a series of physical changes in the body, such as increase in the heart rate increases faster blood flow, ensuring oxygen and nutrients are delivered efficiently to muscles and vital organs. Our breathing quickens to provide more oxygen to the brain, sharpening the focus and reaction time. Blood sugar levels rise as glucose is released into the bloodstream, supplying immediate energy for action. Non-essential functions like digestion, reproduction, and immune activity slow down to conserve energy for critical survival functions. Therefore, we might not want to eat or notice changes in food habits. As the physical changes occur, it enables the person to run (flight) or attack (fight) the situation.

These physiological adjustments developed during the evolution of human species, and historically when faced with predators or dangerous situations, the stress response would enable the person to respond quickly to fight for their basic survival. Often the aspect of "freezing" is commonly liked with more traumatic triggers but also stems from the evolution per se where the individual stands still hoping that the predator moves away. While often when the trigger becomes overwhelming the human response may move from flight or fight (which are commonly seen in stress response) to freeze or flop (i.e. where the body stops being very resistant or flexible to manage the situation). These systems have evolved during modern times and our stress factors have changed accordingly, but the responses are still based on our previous evolutionary experiences or learning and often is an automatic response, unless we consciously learn to change it.

When these changes are triggered repeatedly, without resolution, it often chronically activates our stress response. The trigger, which causes stress over time, may start to be recognised and perceived by our survival system as "threatening" to us – especially if we have not found a way to resolve it, or if there is a lack of capacity to manage it. This then begins to neurologically be perceived as a threat and the same trigger now activates the amygdala (the brain area that perceives fear) as well as the hypothalamus, which already is chronically activated. This overtime switches from being a stressful experience to a more anxiety-provoking experience and may have more long-lasting effects (as discussed in Chapter 1).

THE TWO-SIDED NATURE OF THE STRESS RESPONSE

When we refer to stress the first thing that comes to mind is the negative consequences. While the fight, flight or freeze response is lifesaving in the short term, we have suggested how the prolonged activation of the stress response can cause a multitude of physical health issues within the body. Within our body we have a larger functioning system, referred to as the autonomic nervous system (ANS). The ANS automatically regulates our body processes such as heart rate, digestion, and breathing. This system plays a pivotal role in the stress response.

Within the ANS there are two distinct systems that operate together with the aim of keeping our body regulated. These are: (1) the sympathetic nervous system and (2) the parasympathetic nervous system. The sympathetic nervous system (SNS) which is known as the accelerator, activates the flight or fight system whenever it automatically detects a stress trigger (as detailed above). When this system is operating constantly, it goes into an overdrive leading to wear and tear within the body (also referred to as the allostatic load), which is the cumulative burden of the chronic stress on the physiological system. In individuals who may not have addressed this stress for long periods of time, changing the stress response is not easy and they would need to work with professionals and over time focus on lifestyle changes.

In contrast the parasympathetic nervous system (PNS) works as the break to slow the system down and is activated to promote bodily recovery and overcome the effects one the stressor has passed. The two systems of SNS and PNS work to balance each other. The interplay between the SNS and PNS ensures that the body can respond to stress and then return to a state of equilibrium. However, as the stress becomes chronic, this balance is disrupted, often resulting in insufficient activation of the PNS. This leaves individuals stuck in a heightened state of alertness, unable to relax or recover effectively, which is a result of increased cortisol in the body and often trying to lower this is not easy. It would require the individual to consciously find self-care tools to help down regulate the system where possible.

Understanding how our body responds, helps sense stress even when we may not notice what triggered it or that we are in fact stressed. Now when you notice the changes in your physical body responses such as increased heart rate, sweating hands, stiff neck or tightened muscles you can attribute this to the impact of stress. Which then allows you to "pause" and reflect on what was stressful and how can you regulate it. This pause gives us time to consider and think about the mechanisms that promote self-care to bring our nervous systems back into equilibrium.

Some of us may not necessarily have physical responses but may notice psychological or cognitive changes as the first response to stress. For example, one may become more short-tempered, more anxious or talk a lot more…in other cases one may become more forgetful, find it difficult to multitask, or to pay attention to task that normally does not require a lot of focus. Noticing and recognising these changes allows one to switch from the automatic body responses to being able to find a better solution for self-care and taking a break to help regulate your body from the stressor you might have now recognised.

As the individual experiences chronic stress, there may be a significant toll on different body systems including the cardiovascular system, the immune system, the gastrointestinal system and one's mental health. The elevation of heart rate and blood pressure, meant for short term survival is fine but the continuous activation of this, can lead to long term damage. Over time, individuals may develop a condition of increased high blood pressure (i.e. hypertension), possibly damages to the blood vessels and increases the risk of atherosclerosis (i.e. plaque buildup in arteries), which increases the risks for developing heart attacks and/or strokes. Stress related behaviours may also be visible which includes changes in eating habits (i.e. overeating or not eating), addictions, smoking, alcohol or use of recreational drugs and/or cognitive changes and all of these have long term effects on one's wellbeing.

Cortisol is the primary stress hormone; that has the effect of suppressing immune function especially when present in high concentrations over extended periods of time. While this suppression helps prevent the immune system from overreacting in acute stress situations – which is useful, when stress becomes more chronic the prolonged cortisol production impacts the body, making it vulnerable to infections or inflammation. This could affect many aspects of the body's immune response to infection control and repair, for example wound healing and reducing its ability to fight off diseases or chronic stress related disorders. Eventually this is how stress can lead to more long-term effects such as chronic fatigue syndrome, fibromyalgia, or other autoimmune conditions, which are not easy to recover from without medical and psychological support.

The gut is often referred to as the "second brain," due to the magnitude of nerve endings and its role in balancing the different hormones (e.g. adrenal gland etc.). The gut, located within the structure of the intestinal tract, is known to be profoundly affected by stress. Chronic activation of the stress response affects the hormones in our body which then disturbs the balance of gut bacteria, which negatively affects the digestion, immunity and may lead to conditions such as irritable bowel syndrome (IBS) which alter gut motility, exacerbating symptoms like cramping, diarrhoea, or constipation. Also associated with chronic stress is acid reflux, which refers to the relaxation of the lower oesophageal sphincter (a ring of muscle fibres at the top and bottom of the oesophagus, which is the pipe from the mouth to the stomach) which can cause stomach acid to rise into the oesophagus, resulting in heartburn. Also prolonged stress can disturb the balance of gut bacteria, negatively affecting digestion, immunity, and even mood regulation. Often this impacts the metabolism within one's body and can contribute to changes in blood glucose levels and eventually lead to the type 2 diabetes – which is linked to chronic stress. Changes in the metabolism and the ability to process food within the digestive system and increase in cholesterol can also lead to weight gain.

When the stress is not a distress, but in fact a eustress, it motivates the individual to overcome challenges and use the hormonal change (increase in adrenalin and cortisol levels) to achieve a goal. So, for example, on one hand, if you are anxious to perform well in a job interview – that optimal stress will allow you to prepare and do your homework of learning more about the new company. This allows you to not only improve your understanding and showcase your abilities at the interview but also allows you to focus on practice and building your confidence. This is still a stressful situation, but is within the individual's capacity to manage, therefore the impact of this stress on the body would be minimal and the release of cortisol will reach optimal levels and regulate back quickly. While, on the other hand, if you have a slightly more stressful situation which may be out of your control, for example your significant other has a medical health crisis – and you are balancing the support and the financial goals to survive, you may notice that the arousal and performance curve starts quicker (in the bell curve, see Figure 1.1) compared to a simple stressor (example above). The lack of control in this event will trigger more stress and will have an impact on the body, and your hormones (e.g. cortisol) are released sooner into the body and will take more time to downregulate.

AWARENESS AND COPING: EXPLORING INTERVENTIONS

Firstly, it is important for one to understand the difference between acute and chronic stress. It would help one to also explore the common myths around stress (see Chapter 5 for more details). Once the individual is aware, it allows them to notice the changes in our body whether physical, emotional and/or cognitive. This then provides the opportunity for the person to explore the triggers and understand how to manage the stress for their own self. The key to managing stress is that it should align with the individual's own unique needs and circumstances.

Managing the impact of stress: to effectively manage stress the approach should initially have immediate effects to help the individual cope with the effect of stress. This almost is like the first-aid or quick management response. Then to ensure this is effective over long-term the approach (either the same or a different one) should be aimed at managing the stress triggers over a long-term period. The impact and management of acute stress is very different from managing the long-term effects that one may experience with chronic stress.

On one hand acute stress is where a specific event or trigger is stressful and may cause distress in the individual. Techniques like breathing, being in the moment, physical exercise or movement, using other self-care methods like a bath, or massage, or listening to music etc., would be helpful in giving a bit of relief to the individual at that moment. This will allow the person to pause and respond rather than automatically react to the trigger or the situation. The individual would need to incorporate self-care and learn to be able to use them when faces with a situation that may be acutely stressful. On the other hand, when tackling with chronic stress and its long-term effects, the methods or techniques used for managing will be very different. It may also require quite drastic life-style changes in some cases. Dealing with chronic stress often requires more support and the ability to consistently monitor (for example using stress diaries) and maintain the shift to be able to deal effectively with chronic stress.

SOME USEFUL TECHNIQUES TO MANAGE (ACUTE) STRESS

1) *Harnessing the power of the breath:* Breath is a very good anchor. When we are stressed, our thoughts may often be very negative or

self-criticising. Shifting to your breath, allows you to shift the focus from your thoughts. Noticing the breath and slow or controlled breathing can easily help us regulate from heightened arousal to activating the parasympathetic nervous system which helps us calm our body. There are different methods to help us to use breathing as a technique to calm ourselves.

a. *Diaphragmatic breathing*: This technique involves the individual to use deep, slow breaths that expand the diaphragm. This sends a signal to our body to relax. Studies show positive effect of lowering physiological and psychological stress using diaphragmatic breathing (e.g. Hooper et al., 2019), the time and duration of practising may vary. It would be useful to start a shorter practice (1 to 3 minutes) and eventually increase the time and duration of practice (3 to 5 minutes). To practice this type of breathing, first sit or lie down comfortably. If you are sitting, it's always a good practice to find a place where your legs are firmly placed on the ground (and not hanging in the air). Ideally try not to cross your legs. Place one hand on your chest and the other on your abdomen. Inhale deeply through the nose, allowing the abdomen to rise while the chest remains still. Exhale slowly through the mouth. Repeat this over few times (3 to 5 to begin with and as you practice you can increase this). This also connects your awareness to the shift in your body when inhaling and exhaling.

b. *Box breathing*: This is a popular technique used amongst professionals in high stress environments like athletes and military personnel. It is a simple yet effective method to regain control during stress. To practice this imaging a square (see Figure 2.1) start by following the upper left corner of the square moving towards the upper right, and inhale for up to four counts. So it works something like in (1, 2, 3, 4) and the hold the breath for four counts and you visually move from the upper right corner of the square to the bottom right corner – so you hold (1, 2, 3, 4) and then as you move from bottom right to bottom left – you exhale or breath out for four

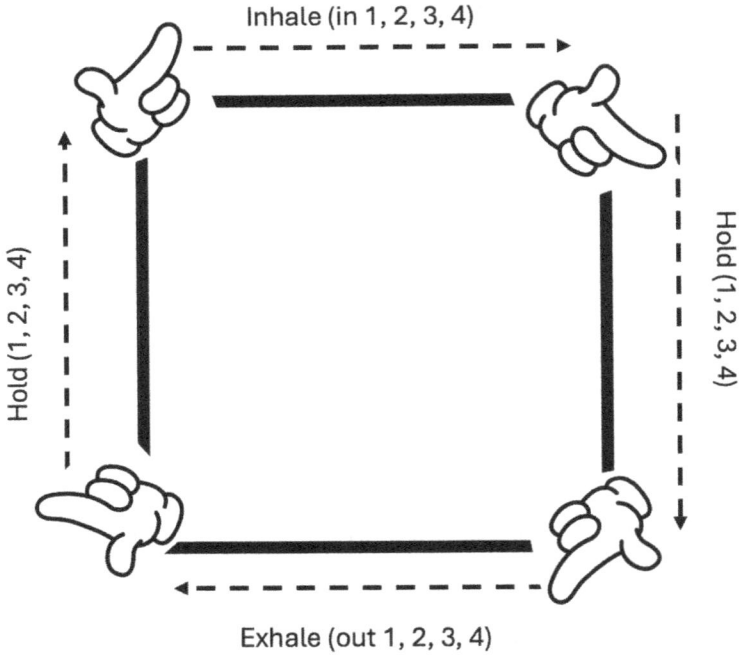

FIGURE 2.1 The box breathing diagram.

counts, so out (1, 2, 3, 4) and then finally as you move from bottom left to upper left corner you hold your breath again for four counts, hold (1, 2, 3, 4). This rhythmic pattern calms the mind and stabilises the heart rate. It is also something that can be used with children, or adolescences as using the diagram helps them follow the box breathing instructions.

c. *Finger breathing also referred to as star breathing:* This is another easy method and can often help you practice this by simply putting your hands under your desk or table when you are with others. To practice this, hold one hand out with the palm facing away from you. Using your other hand start tracing each finger slowly, if you start just below your thumb. Trace each finger up as you breath in and trace each finger down as you breath out. By doing this once, you will have five deep breaths, and you can repeat this a few times.

d. 4-7-8 breathing: This is slightly a more advance method but is known to help you calm down or lower your arousal. To practice this, inhale through your nose for a count of 4, then hold your breath for 7 seconds and exhale through your mouth for 8 seconds. Ideally, you would want to repeat this pattern for at least four times.

e. Pranayama: Is a Sanskrit word and refers to a breathing technique that is grounded in the yogic practice of focusing on the breath. There are different methods associated with this and has different functions. Basic pranayama: is a good starting point. You start by comfortably sitting in a cross-legged position, keep your hands rested on your knees. Remember it's important to listen to your body, if you feel lightheaded or uncomfortable at any point, take a break or return to regular breathing until you are ready to continue. So, start by sitting down and just noticing your regular breathing patterns. If you sit down and notice your breathing, you will know when you are tired or if fatigue has set in and then it's ideal to stop. Slowly allow your breath to become deeper – based on how you feel you may choose to close your eyes or keeping it open. Then slowly take a deep breath through your nose filling your full lungs with air and slowly exhale. Repeat this for a few breaths and focus on the sensation of air moving in and out of your body. Then you go into humming bee breath or Brahmari pranayama. You may close your ears gently with your fingers, when practicing this pranayama. Inhale nicely, while exhaling make that humming sound (hmmm) like a humming bee, make this sound continuously and in a controlled manner. It should not be very loud, but it should create vibration. It would be prolonged slow exhalation, do this up to 5 times (but you can start with 1 or 2 times initially). Breath normally for few minutes and notice the vibrations in your body. Only once you are comfortable, start practicing the basic pranayama and slowly build your stamina to try more advanced breathing exercises. There are many forms of yogic breathing or pranayama techniques, and we have only covered two of the ones. The Bhastrika pranayama: is where you normally sit in a comfortable cross-legged on the floor or a solid surface. If you have difficulty in sitting on the floor, you can use a yoga base or folded blanket at the tip of your spine to give you some support. Rest your hands on your knees. Initially, start with taking few deep breaths to relax your body and mind. Then you begin the practice by inhaling deeply and forcefully through your nose, expanding your chest and abdomen. Exhale is normally forceful and rapid through your nose, drawing your belly towards your spine. Ideally, repeat this rapid breathing initially for 10–15 seconds or until you feel comfortable with the rhythm. It is an advance technique and if you have not done much breathing practices or yoga, you may want to take this slowly and increase your time eventually. Ideally, you could do this practice first thing in the morning, or at a time you are comfortable. If you are not sure, do look up these techniques, which are often easily accessible on YouTube videos or if you practice yoga you can chat with your yoga teacher. If you are prone to migraine, try this technique with some caution, as breathing may trigger feeling a bit uncomfortable. This method is known to have several benefits including respiratory function, boosting metabolism, increasing energy, reducing stress, enhancing mental clarity, balancing the nervous system, improving your immune system and enhancing concentration.

2) *Physical movement as a technique:* Exercise and movement is a very key aspect of our life and is an excellent tool offering immediate and long-term benefits for both body and mind.

a. *Aerobic activities:* is the activity that uses our body's large muscle groups. Often is rhythmic and repetitive. It has been known to directly reduce blood pressure (Hamer et al., 2006). Oxidative stress (OS) is known to play a role in the progression of many aging related diseases. Regular aerobic exercise is known to have a positive effect on the OS level of older adults by reducing oxidant markers and increasing antioxidant marker level (Ye et al., 2021). These include activities like walking, jogging, or cycling which increase endorphin production, the natural chemicals that enhances mood and reduces pain. Yoga, Tai-chi, and Pilates: These practices combine movement with mindfulness, promoting flexibility, balance, and stress relief.

b. *Strength training:* While easily overlooked in discussions of stress management, resistance exercises can reduce symptoms of depression and anxiety. Having high life stressors may lessen your ability to adapt to weight training (Bartholomew et al., 2008). However, evidence suggests that training can not only improve muscle strength and body composition but also improves positive mood and specifically enhance the perception of psychological well-being in older women (Tsutsumi et al., 1998). Therefore, engaging in simple strength training within your homes or training the upper body with resistant bands may be a good beginning. It would help you to seek advice from personal trainers to ensure you engage in safe ways to start strength training.

3) *Mindfulness or other practices:* Mindfulness practice (Kabat-Zinn, 2003, 2015) is thought to be a practice of being in the moment, to bring in non-judgemental awareness into every movement. This is cultivated by paying attention to the present moment and trying to remain non-reactive, non-judgemental and open-hearted as much as possible. Mindfulness initially was adapted from eastern meditative practices but has a more scientific base than any religious underpinning. The idea was to encourage the individual to learn to be in the present moment. As we are aware when we encounter stress, we go into an automatic response of

flight or fight or freeze. While practicing mindfulness has been linked to improve our ability to pause and choose a response and not react automatically to any triggers. Regular practise of mindful meditation has been known to contribute to brain or neural changes. The idea is to not operate in an auto-pilot mode when encountering any triggers. Often it is difficult to bring this into our everyday life, so starting slowly by using short mindfulness practices (3–5 minutes) would be a good way to get into practicing mindfulness and slowly increasing the time and the frequency of weekly practices and engaging with body scans over a period will help integrate the practices. Today, you do have lot of resources on apps or videos on YouTube and you could choose practices which appeal to your senses and use them to guide you.

a. Mindfulness: mindfulness-based approaches like MBSR are known to be more powerful than plain mediation (e.g. Eberth & Sedlmeier, 2012). Evidence suggests that meditation reduces amygdala activity (the brain's fear centre) and enhances prefrontal cortex function, improving emotional regulation and resilience (e.g. Leung et al., 2018; Kwak et al., 2019). There are number of methods to practice mindfulness meditation. But to start with, you want to sit comfortably on a chair or lie on the bed. You can choose to close your eyes or alternatively focus on a point with your eyes half closed. Start by just noticing your breathing, do not try to take deep breaths or manipulate your breathing. Just notice your breath and use it to anchor yourself. As you focus, you may notice your thoughts normally wander or your mind wanders, that is what our brain does, so notice it and gently refocus and bring your attention back to your breathing. Trying not to be critical or judgemental.

b. Body scanning: This form of mindfulness practice involves directing your attention to different parts of the body, gently scanning your body and noticing sensations without reacting to them. It can help release physical tension and promote relaxation. You can start with a 10- or 15-minute body scan and eventually increase the length of your practice.

c. *Visualisation or guided imagery:* This is a method where you create mental image or scenes in your mind to take you to a place where you feel calm. Visualisations can be created to have a safe place, or a walk on the beach and/or any other scenarios. This allows you to not only image the images, but you could make it more vivid by engaging all the senses and immerse yourself in this experience. You could use a guided script to support you. This practice is known to connect your body and mind and can promote relaxation and reduce stress.

d. *Gratitude practices:* are practices focusing on bringing in more gratitude into your awareness and helps to focus on positive aspects of life. Gratitude practices are known to have a range of positive benefits including bringing more joy and pleasure. It reminds us of things that bring a smile and adds value to our life. Existential psychologic often suggests that having a deeper meaning or value helps us cope with existential crises compared to materialistic needs. There are number of ways to become more grateful. You could keep a gratitude journal for instance, where you establish a daily practice to remind yourself of the things you enjoy, the gifts, the grace etc. you can recall and note moments of gratitude with people, think of what made you smile each day. Asking yourself or reflecting on what have you given today? Or what have you received? Or What made me smile today? You could have a gratitude jar where you can put one Post-it note each day with something you feel the gratitude for. You could blog or post on social media for a few days and note the journey.

4) *Building on the strength of social connections:* As humans we are inherently social beings. Having that social connection is often vital for building our resilience. Especially, today in the post-covid world, where social media has caught the attention of the younger generation, although we are often connected socially on social

media and have connections around the world, we often forget the importance of physical connections and intimacy. It is not just romantic pleasures, but meeting a friend for a coffee or walk has benefits beyond words for managing our stress. The ability to talk and share our stress, often helps us process and digest the information and resolve it before it shifts into the chronic stage.

a. *Social media connections:* In today's world most of us are working online in the comfort of our homes. People use Facebook, Snapchat, Instagram, LinkedIn, Twitter (now X) etc. to connect at various levels. Very often we forget that with social media a lot of the content is edited, and we only see one side of the story. It is important for us to remember not to compare ourselves with others but also realise that people seldom share challenges they are going through at that moment.

b. *Emotional support:* We need to find our own connections, this could be friends, family members or someone we can trust to share our concerns or views without the worry of being judged. Sharing concerns with often provides relief and perspective, reducing the emotional burden of stress. In some cultures, like India – people are naturally curious. If you are upset and sit in a cab, you may end up having an open conversation with the cab driver, and being a stranger, this is easy place to be open. In other cultures, you may notice this with hairdressers or barbers where people talk about their life... having a banter over a drink or coffee is also supportive. If it is difficult to find someone in your own life, you could reach out to local support groups which may provide emotional support or look out for other networking events.

c. *Community engagement:* Often being part of local group activities, such as volunteering or joining clubs, fosters a sense of belonging, countering feelings of isolation that stress often exacerbates. Even enrolling in recreational activities or classes for example a gym or a Zumba or Pilate or yoga class or painting or writing groups can give you a sense of being part of a community. You could also explore new hobbies or interest and meet like-minded people.

d. *Professional support*: if you are experiencing chronic stress and struggling to cope, it may be a good idea to seek professional help. You could seek support from psychotherapists or counsellors or psychologists who may be able to provide tailored strategies, emotional support in a more structured framework to help you cope and overcome some of the symptoms and identify your triggers.

5) *Sleep hygiene*: Very often we do not pay attention to sleep patterns and take them for granted. Stress often disrupts sleep patterns. You could have difficulty in falling asleep, have disturbed sleep patterns where you wake up during the night or you may oversleep and still feel tired and fatigued. Ironically, you need adequate rest to recover from your stress. Sleep deprivation can disrupt the body's ability to regulate cortisol and effect one's emotional responses. To help improve your sleep patterns, you could start by maintain your sleep hygiene. It is important to try to refrain from using phone or TV a few hours before your bedtime. It would really help for you to have a regular schedule and try to get to bed around the same time and wake up at a same time to help regulate the body clock or rhythm. Integrating calming bedtime routine like reading, taking a warm bath, or listening to soothing music may help down regulate your body and send a signal the brain that it's time to wind down. It would also help to create a more optimised sleep environment. This may be having a dark, quiet bedroom with the ideal temperature would promote restful sleep. Also, if you can avoid taking work into your bedroom and only using it for sleep often helps you switch off – if you are working at home or are stressed because of work. Having clear boundaries help regulate your ability to switch off. Ideally, 7-9 good hours of sleep is recommended for most adults to manage stress, but you may need 6 – 8 hours or 8 – 10 hours, pay attention to your body and needs.

6) *Balanced nutrition*: Nutrition plays a critical role in our body's ability to recover from stress. Having a balanced diet and noticing any changes in your eating habits would always help you manage your stress or triggers. You want to ensure you have the required carbs, fat and protein along with other antioxidant rich food in your diet. Pay attention to your caffeine intake and/or alcohol intake, as this may contribute to managing your stress or affect your sleep patterns. Dehydration can exacerbate stress symptoms, so it is important to ensure you have plenty of water to manage your hydration, especially when you are also working on physical exercises or movements.

7) *A holistic approach*: Although each of the aspect above are ideal on their own, the key to managing stress is in integrating all the approaches and taking a more holistic approach. Especially, when managing chronic stress, it requires you to make significant life-changes and it is important to look at the subjective wellbeing but also integrate the physical (understanding your rhythm, and being able to regulate and restore this), psychological (the understanding of your mind and your mental health), social (connecting with your network from a relationship perse and connecting with compassion), and the spiritual self (accessing your own connection beyond – this could be your beliefs, religion or practices which allow you to find the inner strength).

These techniques have been introduced to you here in this chapter to allow you to hold in mind what might work best for you, in the particular circumstances you are in, to start to become aware of where you hold your stress in your bodily system and how you can engage your parasympathetic response to allow it to balance an overactive sympathetic system. As mentioned, we are all unique and your preferred technique to engage calm will be different, therefore we do not suggest you need to do all the aspects shown here! Pick and choose what works for you to notice the impact of your stress and reduce the impact on your body by tuning in to it. Using the understanding of the physical and mental aspects of stress and the different coping mechanisms, the next chapter will explore the role of neurodiversity, culture and ethnic contexts in experience and management of stress.

3

NEURODIVERSE, CULTURAL, AND ETHNIC PERSPECTIVE IN STRESS

This chapter focuses on the understanding of the term neurodiversity and whether neurodivergent individuals might be more likely to suffer stress than neurotypical individuals and thinking about how to cope with stress from a neurodiverse perspective. Awareness of the human brain and its connectivity can often also help individuals and professionals understand why they respond in a particular way and learn to change their behaviour. The chapter further integrates aspects of cultural and ethical perspectives around stress that may stem from the common practices or historical aspects.

WHAT IS NEURODIVERSITY AND HOW IS IT RELATED TO STRESS?

Neurodiversity, or what was known as neurodivergent, was a term first used in the 1990s. The idea of the term neurodiversity emphasises on the idea that as humans our brains are different in the way it processes information and learns. There is no "right" way of thinking, learning or processing information and these differences are not viewed as deficits or impairment. Under the umbrella term of neurodiversity, you have several neurological or development conditions

DOI: 10.4324/9781003537410-3

including autism spectrum disorder (ASD), attention deficit hyperactivity disorder (ADHD), dyslexia, dyspraxia, obsessive compulsive disorders (OCD) and many others. The neurodiversity concept challenges the traditional medical model that seeks to "cure" these conditions, instead suggesting advocating and understanding for embracing different ways of being. Neurodiversity acknowledges that everyone thinks and experiences the world uniquely, and it is important to understand this especially when thinking about supporting stress management and coping techniques which might need to be flexible.

Research suggests that neurodivergent individuals also encounter triggers and factors that may trigger stressors. However, there is evidence that to work through challenges, it is important to have a more collaborative approach between professionals and neurodiverse to develop a meaningful and effective shift. Within the range of neurodiversity conditions, there are number of processes that may be different compared to individuals without the conditions. Sensory processing differences are an often noticed in more than one neurodivergent condition. Individuals who have sensory processing difficulties often experience heightened sensitivity within the environment for loud noises, bright lights, or crowded spaces, which is quite overwhelming, but may be ok for someone without neurodiversity. This aspect of being easily overwhelmed can make simple daily activities, such as shopping or commuting, extremely stressful. People may find a bustling office environment with fluorescent lighting and constant background noise might not be noticed by neurotypical employees, but it could be very distressing for a neurodivergent person. Similarly, they may find unplanned activity difficult to engage with, as multitasking is often quite stressful and can add to the sense of being overwhelmed. This heightened arousal triggered by sensory overload can result in elevated cortisol levels, and over time contribute to chronic stress.

Again, social challenges faced by neurodivergent individuals often may stem from lack of awareness within the larger society. Often the pressures of fitting into the societal expectation also leads to feelings of alienation and marginalisation. Neurodiverse individuals often mask their natural behaviours or thoughts to align with the societal expectation this process can be both exhausting and detrimental to their mental health. Most of our current world has been designed keeping neurotypical people in mind, this coupled with the sensory overload, and masking can place a heavy cognitive burden on neurodivergent individuals. The effort required to navigate environments and tasks that do not naturally align with their abilities, leads to regular mental exhaustion and burnout. For example, an adult with dyslexia may need to spend considerable extra time decoding written instructions, taking significantly more energy and time than their peers to complete the same task. This constant demand for additional effort highlights the systemic inequities that exacerbates stress for neurodivergent individuals.

There is a need to understand and manage expectation and in early years, avoid labelling of behaviour. A classic example is someone with ADHD may find it difficult to remain seated and focus for long periods of time and often may want to take breaks and often this gets the individual labelled as disruptive and can have a detrimental effect on the individual's self-esteem and reinforce feelings of inadequacy and stress. Often, this coupled with their own internal scripts, there may be a lot of self-doubt leading to higher risk for these individuals to experience stress. Specifically, with the interplay between neurological differences and existing societal expectations creates higher vulnerabilities for neurodivergent individuals. There is research evidence suggesting there may be differences in frontal networks and the default mode networks for individuals with autism conditions and ADHD (Hutson & Hutson, 2024). Neuroscience evidence (Rowland, 2024) also suggests that a dysfunctional cingulate gyrus hyperfocuses attention in the left frontal lobe with lower ability to access the right frontal lobe. This often affects the ability to be spontaneous and the social behaviour. Often someone with autism for example may have reduced functioning of amygdala and there for may not feel emotion or experience fear but often process their emotions more intellectually. So, within a therapeutic setting for example, dealing with emotions in neurodiverse individuals may be more difficult as they could tend to intellectualise the feeling or emotion rather than to feel it in their body, so the focus of the work may need to initially link what they notice in their bodily sensations and any changes they observe to how they "label" their feelings, and then use that to connect with their emotions to help them to recognise a range of different states, that will include stress, anxiety, anger, sadness, happiness and joy amongst others.

Internalised stigma also plays a critical role in increasing stress vulnerability. Societal attitudes toward neurodivergence often carry negative connotations, leading many neurodivergent individuals to internalise these perceptions. As a result, they may experience feelings of inadequacy, low self-esteem, and shame. This internalised stigma not only affects mental well-being but also increases susceptibility to stress-related conditions such as anxiety and depression. Stress levels are often further exacerbated by the presence of comorbid conditions, which are common among neurodivergent individuals. For example, those with ADHD may struggle to focus or plan their schedule and have quite a few uncompleted tasks which would lead to chronic worry and anxiety. These ongoing challenges create a cycle with stress feeding into anxiety and vice versa, the ability to manage and break out of this could be quite challenging without relevant support networks or professional inputs.

ADAPTING THE STRATEGIES: BRINGING IN THE NEURODIVERSE PERSPECTIVE

The strategies mentioned in Chapter 2, can be adapted, but the most important aspect when adapting the strategies, is to collaborate and check in with the individual. As it has been seen, the engagement and adherence in using these strategies are better when individuals co-create or co-design them. For example, when using visualisation – a client of mine (SF) would want to chip in to the guided visualisation. So, we would agree what imagery the client preferred, and SF would prompt something along lines, of walking on the sand by the beach…the client will then continue on saying something like, there was a lovely butterfly, and the sound of the waves was mesmerizing.

Along with having a more collaborative approach, working with individuals who may have traits of neurodiversity would need to have a friendly and less cluttered environment. Ensuring spaces have good sound proofing and have adjustable lights create a more comfortable environment and reduces the sensory overload. Which further allows them to engage in coping strategies. Finally raising more awareness about neurodiversity, engaging with companies and local service providers and advocating for changes to help individuals with neurodiversity often directly reduces stigma, allowing the individual to be themselves and over time fosters a more supporting and non-judgmental environment with better inclusivity.

THE ROLE OF CULTURE IN STRESS

Stress does not exist in a *vacuum*, it is embedded within the social, cultural environments we live. Our relationships right from the early childhood days, the cultural values we grew up in, the current cultural values and practices and societal structures plan significant roles in shaping how we perceive and learn to experience stress and cope with it and continues to shape our learning consistently. The previous experience may have been more conducive for our coping and migrating to a new culture or society nationally or internationally may make us more vulnerable to stress and affect our coping.

For example, having been born in a city in Mumbai India SF has grown up learning to challenge belief systems and comes from a more open Indian culture, SF was also in an Irish Convent School so the resilience and discipline and curiosity to be open to life experiences was very different during early childhood periods. As she became an adult, she lived in few other cities around India, if the society was a bit more traditional in their approach, it was often a stress and took time for SF to adapt to the lifestyle and expectations. Similarly, having travelled across continents – it was very important for SF to develop a coping strategy that was more flexible and have a network of good social support both in the city or country she lived in to learn about the expectations and cultures, but also continued to keep in touch with friends from India who continued to provide that support both emotionally and intellectually.

Social networks can serve as powerful buffers against stress, but coming to a new country when you have not travelled before can be very intimidating. Especially, this is seen in universities and global companies where international students or colleagues often take time to acclimatise to the culture, learn the etiquette and the culture of the new place. Often a lot of importance is given to orientation programs that help people travelling to know more about the cultures. Having a supportive group of friends, family members, or colleagues can provide emotional reassurance, practical assistance, and a sense of belonging that eases the burden of stress. When there is a sense of feeling validated and understood by those around us, our capacity to navigate challenges increases because the self-confidence and resilience increases, and the self-doubt reduces. On the other hand, being alone and feeling unsupported or unheard can increase the sense of being overwhelmed. Not having a social network or a buffer can amplify the sense of vulnerability especially during challenging times. In today's work with the social networks and connection – it is easier to try to keep the social connections alive and use it to thrive in challenging situations.

When the individual is in a country and notices that they are in the minority, there is a lack of belongingness that often is quite stark. Which can be overwhelming whilst also adjusting to the cultural practices. Having experience of working in the HEA setting, and engaging with mobility programs within UK and India, students find it easier to adapt when they have a buddy from the host country. That sense of having a buddy, though takes a bit of time – the relationship develops to having a trusted friend who can answer awkward questions about the culture, without having the worry of being labelled as a "racist" comment. To be able to navigate stress from a cultural perspective, it is important to be open, curious, have a need to learn and observe the practices. Most importantly to be compassionate you your own self, as you will learn and will make mistakes and navigate through the cultural perspective.

Cultural norms and expectations play an important role in shaping the way stress is perceived and manifested. In some cultures, including South Asia, Africa and some European countries – food is a very easy way to cope with stress. The community thrives in sharing of the practices be it a cup of tea (in England), a conversation of chai (in India) or a banter over a pint or a nice glass of wine. These are ways to welcome others into the culture and share something that is close and personal. Societies also have a collectivist or an individualistic culture and migrating between the two can be very challenging and create more acute or even chronic stress. In collectivist cultures, where community and familial obligations are highly valued, stress often arises from the pressures to meet these shared responsibilities. The expectations to achieve are often driven into the individuals from very early childhood and not achieving the goals sometime is not an option in that individual's mind. Based on the internal scripts, the individual may associate feelings of shame, guilt or not being good enough if they perform below the expectations. This internal dilemma or script continues to become part of the self-talk as an adult and when they fail to meet this expectation there may be a lot of stress and feelings of failure associated with this. Collectivist societies, such as those in many Asian, African, and Latin American countries, prioritise the group over the individual. Family, community, and societal harmony are central values, and stress often arises from a sense of obligation to uphold these bonds. Family expectations, obligations to group adherences and stigma to mental health issues – due to lack of awareness, or existing cultural beliefs can often be key sources of stress. The perception of how we present to the society is given a lot of value and importance. So, seeking help for emotional struggles or opening up to the difficulties one may be experiencing is often perceived as a failure and is not shared in some cultures.

While individualistic cultures place a higher emphasis on personal achievement and autonomy. In contrast, individualist cultures, such as those in Western Europe and North America, emphasise personal freedom, autonomy, and achievement. Stress in these societies often stems from the pressure to excel independently and "stand out" from the crowd. Children are encouraged to be independent from day one and expected to have their own place as they become adults, compared to the collective cultures where the idea is to have more joint families and children often live under the same roof. Within individualistic cultures, loneliness, fear of failure and trying to achieve a work-life balance can be sources of stress. But the relentless pursuit of success and the expectation of self-reliance, where they have learnt to only rely on themselves, individuals struggle to reach out for help and work independently in resolving any crisis until they reach a point of breakdown to realise there is help and support available.

Socioeconomic factors play a critical role to this complex equation. Financial insecurity, job instability, and limited access to resources create a pervasive undercurrent of stress that can overshadow other life challenges. For individuals from marginalised groups, these stressors are often compounded by systemic inequities and discrimination. The chronic stress of navigating unequal opportunities, microaggressions, or outright prejudice can have profound and lasting effects on both mental and physical wellbeing. Often the drive is to continuously meet the financial threshold to be able to reach an equilibrium, but with stress reaching that may be difficult. Understanding the interplay between social and cultural influences is crucial when planning strategies to cope and manage stress. Recognising that stress may be a personal experience but there may be broader societal, cultural and environmental factors contributing to the perception of stress, allows us to approach it with greater empathy and awareness.

Culture profoundly influences how stress is perceived and managed. It shapes our beliefs about what constitutes stress and the acceptable ways of coping with stress as well as the resources available to address stressors. Cultural background not only affects an individual's responses to stress but also determines societal attitudes towards mental health. Cultural attitudes toward mental health can either exacerbate or mitigate stress. In many collectivist societies, seeking mental health care is taboo, viewed as a sign of weakness or failure. Conversely, some cultural frameworks normalise stress as a part of life, promoting resilience through traditional practices.

DE-COLONISING THE UNDERSTANDING OF STRESS

Communities with a history of colonisation, slavery, or forced displacement may carry psychological wounds that are transmitted across generations. For instance, Indigenous populations in North America and Australia frequently face high rates of stress-related conditions, because of the lingering effects of colonisation and the loss of autonomy. Similarly, descendants of enslaved peoples often experience heightened stress due to systemic racism and economic disparities that persist in contemporary society. This generational transmission of trauma underscores how historical events continue to influence present-day mental health. Especially, if individuals travel from these communities that were colonised to countries who colonised them. We often forget the role of colonisation and history. For example, having a conversation with someone who was travelling from UK to India, and was in their early 20s were surprised to hear about the history of England with India till they read about it. However, growing up in India we often talked and learned about the historical perspectives and the story of Indian independence. Being aware and curios often allows us to work with individuals and their whole experience.

Unfortunately, within published work and research most of the work in stress perceptions and managing and coping styles have been historically dominated by Western models, which often prioritise individualism and clinical interventions. While effective in some contexts, these approaches may fail to serve the needs of a diverse global population. Western approaches to stress management often face significant limitations when applied universally, as they are deeply rooted in individualistic frameworks that may not align with the lived experiences of people from diverse cultural backgrounds. Stress management strategies in these frameworks typically emphasise personal responsibility, such as practicing self-care, engaging in mindfulness, or seeking therapy. While these techniques can be effective, they often overlook the communal or relational dimensions of stress that are central to many cultures. For individuals from collectivist societies, the focus on personal autonomy may feel disconnected from their experiences, where stress is often seen as shared or influenced by family and the community.

Another challenge with the western models is the concept of labelling emotional states such as sadness, anxiety, or anger as symptoms of a disorder, emphasising the need for diagnosis and treatment. However, in many cultures, these emotions are viewed as natural, transient responses to life events or even as opportunities for spiritual growth and transformation. These practices or beliefs are not explored sufficiently to be yet fully integrated into western models, but there is a disconnection between the two worlds. This gap needs to reduce, and we must be more integrative in our approaches and honour cultural interpretations of emotional experiences.

Western frameworks often exhibit blind spots, neglecting historical factors that contribute to stress. Issues such as colonisation, economic inequities, and cultural dislocation are rarely addressed in mainstream models. By focusing narrowly on individual factors, these models risk ignoring the broader social and historical contexts that can shape stress. To create a more inclusive and effective approach, it is essential to acknowledge and address these limitations. Decolonising the understanding of stress involves acknowledging the limitations of these frameworks, integrating holistic and non-western traditions, and valuing diverse perspectives on emotional experiences and coping mechanisms. It has only been in the recent two decades a lot of eastern philosophy, and wisdom is being used in mainstream stress management workshops. With the evidence now given to mindfulness practice, which stems from eastern meditation practices but has been adapted to a more scientific framework, holistic approaches are now entering the mainstream of coping strategies. More recently within global leadership and stress management training a lot of focus has been given to aspects of flourishing which goes beyond basic management of stressful triggers but having a more holistic perspective of better quality of life and having a more balance work-life perspective. The aspect of thriving and flourishing also integrates aspects of different cultural perspectives but is aimed at making more long-term changes in individuals and organisations.

REFRAMING STRESS NARRATIVES

Reframing stress narratives involves decolonising the understanding of stress by questioning dominant frameworks and embracing diverse perspectives that reflect the lived experiences of global populations. This process calls for a shift away from existing western models but creating a more integrative model which is more inclusive. Often it feels easier to use existing framework and adapt it to cultural and wider context, but this approach may not be robust enough. Acknowledging diverse views of stress is an essential step to support this new framework. In many Indigenous traditions, stress is not merely a psychological or physiological issue but may be seen as a misalignment with natural or spiritual forces. Similarly, African, and Caribbean communities often place a strong emphasis on spirituality and communal support as central components of stress management. These perspectives highlight the relationship between individuals, their communities, and the world around them. Understanding the different perspectives of stress and tailoring coping strategies to the cultural contexts of participants ensures that they incorporate local traditions. By respecting cultural norms and values, stress management programs can feel more relevant and accessible, increasing the likelihood of their success. Ongoing exposure to prejudice undermines well-being and exacerbates existing vulnerabilities. Economic disparities further amplify these challenges, as limited access to education, healthcare, and economic opportunities imposes financial strain. Cultural dissonance is another source of stress, particularly for immigrants or children of immigrants, who often feel torn between preserving their cultural identity and assimilating into the dominant culture. This internal conflict can undermine mental health, as individuals navigate dual expectations and struggle with belonging.

Normalising emotional experiences is another important aspect of reframing stress. Many non-western culture's view emotions such as sadness, fear, or anger as natural parts of the human experience rather than conditions requiring intervention. This approach encourages acceptance and compassion, helping individuals embrace their emotional states without judgment. Challenging the cause of stress allows it to be reframed from being a "problem to be solved" into an opportunity for growth, balance, or spiritual awakening. Integrating non-western perspectives into stress narratives broadens the understanding of stress, creating space for healing practices that align with diverse cultural values and traditions. This reframing fosters a more inclusive and compassionate approach to managing stress. These historical and systemic stressors highlight the need for an understanding of how ethnic and cultural factors intersect with stress, emphasising the importance of addressing these issues within broader societal and therapeutic frameworks.

BRINGING THE PERSPECTIVES TOGETHER

Stress becomes significantly magnified when biases intersect with personal challenges. For instance, a neurodivergent individual from a marginalised ethnic group may face the dual pressures of racism and discrimination alongside challenges related to heightened sensory stimulus. The need to navigate these combined pressures can create a continuous state of heightened stress, which can result in mental and physical health issues. This compounded stress highlights the complexity of multiple identities and the extra burdens they place on individuals. While overlapping identities can amplify stress, they can also serve as a source of resilience by providing access to diverse coping strategies. A neurodivergent individual from a collectivist culture might draw strength from community-based mechanisms such as family support or participation in cultural rituals. These collective approaches can complement strategies like mindfulness, which may be adapted to suit their unique sensory needs. The interplay of cultural and personal resources underscores the potential for resilience within intersectional identities, even amid significant stressors.

Tailoring stress management techniques to an individual's unique neurobiological and cultural context is essential for fostering inclusivity. Recognising and accommodating the diversity of stress responses allows for more personalised and meaningful interventions, reducing stress and enhancing overall well-being. Stress management becomes particularly effective when coping strategies consider both neurodiversity and cultural context. For instance, a child with ADHD from a Latino family might benefit from structured routines that incorporate culturally meaningful activities, such as music or dance, to foster engagement and reduce stress. Similarly, an autistic adult in a collectivist culture may find comfort in small group mindfulness sessions that emphasise community over individual focus, aligning with their cultural values. By blending neurobiological and cultural considerations, stress management strategies can be tailored to the individual, resulting in more holistic and effective outcomes.

Inclusive coping strategies are essential for addressing the diverse needs of individuals and fostering environments where everyone can thrive. Achieving this inclusivity often requires systemic changes that go beyond individual interventions to create broader societal support. Community education and awareness programs plays a vital role in promoting inclusivity. Raising awareness about neurodiversity and cultural sensitivity helps to combat any stigma and foster understanding. By educating communities, society can move toward greater acceptance of differences, reducing the social pressures that contribute to stress. Advocating for policy changes is a critical step in reducing systemic stressors. Policies in workplaces, schools, and healthcare settings should be designed to accommodate diverse needs, ensuring that everyone has equal access to resources and opportunities. Inclusive policies might include flexible work arrangements, culturally competent healthcare, and education systems that recognise and support neurodivergent learners. Empowering individuals to understand their unique stress profiles, whether shaped by neurodiversity, cultural identity, or both, enables them to regain control over their coping strategies. Providing tools, resources, and safe spaces where diverse people are acknowledged and respected can significantly enhance resilience and overall well-being. Stress is an undeniable and universal human experience, the manifestations, causes, and impacts are deeply influenced by the unique neurobiological, cultural, and historical contexts of individuals and communities. This diversity highlights the importance of recognising the varied ways in which stress is experienced, understood, and managed across different populations.

4

ROLE OF MOVEMENT IN MANAGING STRESS

We are often aware of several methods that one may engage in to deal with stress. This may have come from reading around methods, hearing various advice from people or society. In this chapter we focus on how movement specifically supports recovery from stress. We will discuss how movement can affect our brain chemistry and in turn these chemicals make us feel better. We would also discuss the underlying principles of the eastern philosophies (e.g., yoga, meditation, Pilates, and breathing) and how they have evolved to support movement in therapy. This is also very useful when we look at stress caused by more adverse trauma. Stress and unresolved emotional issues have a somatic response within our bodies, we will explore the use of movement to overcome these feelings and relieve the symptoms of stress.

ROLE OF MOVEMENT IN MANAGING STRESS

As we have learnt in earlier chapters stress, in many ways, manifests physically as much as it does mentally. Our muscles tense, our heart rate increases, and the body prepares itself for action—this is commonly known as the "fight-or-flight" response. Over time, if the physical response is repeated, the body can experience chronic

DOI: 10.4324/9781003537410-4

stress and, if left unresolved, these physical manifestations can lead to fatigue, tension, and even illness. In this chapter, we explore how movement plays a critical role in managing and alleviating stress. By understanding the connection between the body and the mind, and how movement impacts brain chemistry, we can appreciate why even simple movements can make a significant difference to our well-being.

The connection between movement and stress relief

Movement means different things to different people. For some, it may evoke memories of enjoyable activities like dance or sports, while others may recall physical exercise sessions at school as traumatic or frustrating. These early experiences shape how we relate to movement as adults, but what is often overlooked is the profound therapeutic potential of simple physical activities. Movement, whether large or small, plays a significant role in emotional and mental well-being. Movement helps the brain regulate key neurotransmitters, including serotonin, dopamine, and endorphins. These chemicals play a critical role in how we feel and function daily. Research has shown that regular physical activity can reduce anxiety and depression by triggering the release of these feel-good chemicals, often improving mood and cognitive function. For example, a large study conducted by Chekroud et al. (2018), published in *The Lancet Psychiatry*, found that people who exercised had 43% fewer days of poor mental health each month compared to those who did not exercise. Importantly, the study included all kinds of physical activity, from walking and yoga to sports, highlighting that any movement, even low intensity, significantly impacts mental well-being. In addition to enhancing mental clarity, movement shifts our focus away from stress-inducing thoughts to the sensations in our body, allowing us to redirect attention toward more positive experiences. This process is often referred to as "embodied cognition," where the physical state of our body influences our thoughts and emotions. By engaging in movement, we break the feedback loop of stress and negative thinking, creating space for more adaptive cognitive processes.

As noted in McGonigal's (2019) *The Joy of Movement*, physical activities foster a sense of belonging and hope, allowing us to transcend negative emotions. She emphasises that movement can be a source of identity, community, and joy—elements that are particularly vital in overcoming feelings of isolation and stress. Her work highlights how exercise helps shift perspective and provides a sense of control over one's emotions, thus creating a healthier, more balanced outlook on life.

The role of movement in reducing chronic stress and inflammation

Chronic stress doesn't just impact the mind; it can also trigger physical inflammation throughout the body. When we experience stress, the immune system releases pro-inflammatory cytokines, which, in the short term, are meant to protect the body from harm. However, when stress becomes prolonged, this inflammatory response can contribute to a host of health problems, including heart disease, diabetes, gastro-intestinal and autoimmune disorders. Chronic inflammation also plays a role in mental health conditions like depression and anxiety, creating a feedback loop where stress leads to inflammation, which then exacerbates stress. Movement, especially regular aerobic exercise, has been shown to reduce inflammation by lowering the levels of pro-inflammatory markers in the body. Aerobic exercise refers to what is commonly also known as cardio. It includes exercises like brisk walking, swimming, running etc. It activates the heart rate and breathing, while also using the body's large muscles. Engaging in physical activity helps regulate the immune system's response, reducing excessive inflammation and promoting overall health. Studies have demonstrated that individuals who engage in consistent moderate to intense exercise experience lower levels of inflammation, even when faced with stressful life events.

Pilates, yoga and tai chi, which combine gentle movement with mindfulness and breathwork, are also effective in reducing both stress and inflammation. These practices promote relaxation and balance within the autonomic nervous system, shifting the body away from the "fight-or-flight" response and into the "rest-and-digest" mode, where healing and recovery take place. This relaxation response has been associated with lower levels of C-reactive protein (CRP), an inflammatory marker commonly linked to chronic stress and cardiovascular disease. By reducing inflammation, movement not only helps alleviate stress in the short term but also protects the body from the long-term health consequences of chronic stress.

The social aspect of movement: building a support system

Another powerful dimension of movement is its capacity to foster social connections, which are crucial for managing stress. Humans are inherently social creatures, and isolation can exacerbate feelings of stress, anxiety, and depression. Engaging in group activities, such as team sports, fitness classes, or even group walks, provides a sense of community and belonging that can buffer against the effects of stress. Social interactions during physical activities can enhance motivation, accountability, and enjoyment, making it easier to stick to a regular movement routine. Research suggests that exercising in a group setting can enhance the release of endorphins beyond what is typically experienced when exercising alone. This "collective euphoria," often felt during group fitness classes or team sports, fosters feelings of social bonding and improves mood. Additionally, exercising with others can reduce the perceived effort of the activity, making it feel more enjoyable and less daunting. Whether it's joining a local running club, participating in a dance class, or simply walking with friends, incorporating social elements into movement can greatly enhance its stress-relieving effects.

For individuals who may feel self-conscious or reluctant to engage in physical activity alone, group exercise offers a supportive environment that promotes not only physical health but also emotional well-being. The shared experience of overcoming physical challenges together fosters a sense of camaraderie and mutual encouragement, helping individuals build emotional resilience while also improving their fitness.

Movement and brain chemistry: how exercise affects the mind

At its core, movement affects our brain chemistry in ways that directly counteract the effects of stress. Stress activates the hypothalamic-pituitary-adrenal (HPA) axis, leading to the release of cortisol, a hormone that prepares the body for immediate action. While beneficial in short bursts, chronic exposure to elevated cortisol levels can harm both physical and mental health. Exercise, especially aerobic activity, helps regulate the release of cortisol and stimulates the production of endorphins—neurotransmitters often referred to as the brain's natural painkillers. Endorphins produce feelings of euphoria and general well-being, reducing the perception of pain and enhancing mood. Research by Ströhle (2009) suggests that exercise is as effective as antidepressants in treating mild to moderate depression, as it triggers the release of these chemicals that naturally elevate mood.

Regular physical activity also increases levels of dopamine, a neurotransmitter associated with reward and motivation, which can help individuals feel more driven and focused. This is particularly important for individuals suffering from stress-induced fatigue or lack of motivation, as movement can re-engage the brain's reward systems, providing a much-needed sense of accomplishment and pleasure.

A study by Cotman and Berchtold (2002) demonstrates how exercise triggers neuroplasticity—the brain's ability to reorganise and form new neural connections. This is particularly relevant for individuals dealing with chronic stress, anxiety, or trauma, as the brain's ability to adapt to new information is crucial for long-term emotional resilience. Movement-based activities such as yoga, tai chi, and even walking can help foster this neuroplasticity, offering the brain a chance to reset and recover from the harmful effects of prolonged stress.

Movement and mind-body integration

A growing body of research supports the idea that movement is most effective in managing stress when it incorporates both physical and mental elements. Mind-body integration practices like yoga, tai chi, and Pilates exemplify this approach, combining physical movement with mental focus and breath control. These practices help individuals develop a deeper awareness of their bodies and minds, fostering a sense of harmony that counteracts the fragmented feeling often associated with chronic stress.

Mind-body practices work by activating the parasympathetic nervous system, which promotes relaxation and recovery. This is the opposite of the stress response, which is governed by the sympathetic nervous system. Regular engagement in mind-body activities helps "train" the nervous system to recover more quickly from stress, making it easier to maintain emotional balance even in the face of challenging situations. Moreover, these practices emphasise the importance of intentionality in movement. Rather than exercising purely for physical fitness, mind-body practices encourage individuals to move with mindfulness and purpose, focusing on the sensations of the body and the flow of the breath. This creates a more holistic approach to movement, where the goal is not just physical strength or endurance but also mental clarity, emotional balance, and inner peace.

MOVEMENT IN EASTERN PHILOSOPHIES: YOGA, MEDITATION, AND BREATHWORK

Eastern philosophies like yoga, tai chi, have long integrated movement with mindfulness, offering not only physical benefits but also mental and emotional healing. These practices combine breath control, deliberate movement, and meditative focus to align the body and mind. The gentle, flowing movements in practices like tai chi help release tension stored in the body, promoting relaxation and stress relief. Yoga has gained widespread recognition for its role in stress management. Studies have shown that yoga reduces cortisol levels and enhances parasympathetic nervous system activity, which helps calm the body after stress. The combination of physical postures (asanas), controlled breathing (pranayama), and meditation helps individuals become more mindful of their bodies and emotions. This mindfulness helps individuals identify stress triggers and respond to them with greater awareness, reducing the automatic "fight-or-flight" response.

Pilates, though originally developed for physical rehabilitation, has also been shown to help individuals manage stress by focusing on controlled, precise movements that enhance physical strength and flexibility. Pilates emphasises core stabilisation, which not only strengthens the body but also improves balance and coordination, both of which can increase self-confidence and reduce stress-related anxiety. Breathwork, a key component of both yoga, meditation, and Pilates, has also proven to be a powerful tool in managing stress. Deep, diaphragmatic breathing activates the parasympathetic nervous system, often referred to as the "rest and digest" system. This shifts the body out of a stress response, reducing heart rate and lowering blood pressure. Incorporating breathwork into daily routines, whether through structured exercises or mindful breathing during moments of stress, can lead to significant improvements in emotional regulation.

THE SOMATIC EXPERIENCE: HOW MOVEMENT HELPS PROCESS EMOTIONS

Stress is not only a mental experience; it is somatic, meaning it is stored in the body. Somatic stress refers to the physical sensations that arise from emotional or psychological tension. This can manifest as muscle tension, headaches, digestive issues, or even chronic pain. Often, the body holds onto unresolved emotions, leading to a cycle of discomfort and stress that can be difficult to break. The concept of the "body keeps the score," as coined by psychiatrist Van der Kolk (2014), emphasises that traumatic or stressful experiences often leave imprints on the body, which must be addressed as part of healing. Movement plays a critical role in helping release these pent-up emotions and physical sensations. For instance, trauma-informed movement therapies, such as trauma-sensitive yoga or somatic experiencing therapy, focus on helping individuals reconnect with their bodies in a safe and controlled way. These practices help people understand the physical manifestations of their stress and how movement can facilitate the release of those emotions. Trauma-sensitive yoga is designed to help individuals gently explore their bodies' responses to stress, allowing for a gradual release of tension and a better understanding of how trauma affects the body.

By becoming more attuned to the body's signals, individuals can better identify when they are experiencing stress and take steps to alleviate it through movement. This awareness, sometimes referred to as "interoception," is the body's ability to sense its internal state, and it plays a significant role in emotional regulation. Research has shown that individuals with higher interoceptive awareness are better able to manage stress and emotional challenges because they are more in tune with their body's needs and responses (Porges, 2011).

Moreover, movement therapies like dance and expressive movement provide an outlet for individuals to externalise their emotions. Dance has long been used as a form of emotional expression, dating back to ancient rituals that used movement to communicate joy, grief, or celebration. In modern expressive movement therapies, individuals are encouraged to move freely in response to their emotions, allowing them to process feelings that may be difficult to articulate in words. This form of non-verbal communication offers a valuable means of stress relief, especially for those who find it challenging to express their emotions verbally.

Dance Movement Psychotherapy (DMP), as a therapeutic practice, is grounded in the belief that movement and emotion are interconnected. It is especially effective for people who have experienced trauma or chronic stress, as it helps them reconnect with their bodies in a non-judgmental, supportive environment. Studies have shown that DMP can reduce anxiety and depression, improve body image, and enhance emotional resilience. McGonigal's research emphasises that moving in sync with others—whether in a dance class, yoga group, or even walking with a friend—can enhance social bonding, reduce feelings of isolation, and increase the release of mood-enhancing chemicals like dopamine and oxytocin. This form of synchronised movement reminds us of our evolutionary heritage, where group cohesion and collective movement were essential for survival, fostering a deep sense of connection and well-being.

BUILDING RESILIENCE AND CONFIDENCE THROUGH MOVEMENT

The act of moving, especially when done consistently, builds both physical and emotional resilience. Resilience is the ability to recover from setbacks and adapt to challenging situations. Through movement, individuals can cultivate a sense of control over their bodies, which in turn enhances their confidence in managing stress. When people move outside in nature, this can further boost resilience. Activities such as hiking, running, or even mindful walking in a natural environment provide dual benefits: the physical challenge of movement combined with the calming effects of being in nature. Research conducted by Bratman et al. (2015) found that people who walked in nature for 90 minutes showed decreased activity in the part of the brain associated with repetitive negative thinking, a hallmark of stress and depression. This suggests that combining movement with exposure to nature amplifies the stress-relieving benefits of physical activity. Additionally, overcoming physical challenges, such as completing a difficult hike or mastering a yoga pose, can instil a sense of accomplishment and empowerment. When your body proves that it can meet physical challenges, the mind often follows, helping to reinforce a mindset of strength and resilience. Resilience is not only built through the physical act of movement but also through the psychological benefits that movement fosters. As individuals see progress in their physical abilities—whether it's completing a workout or simply feeling more flexible—they also begin to feel more capable of handling stress. This improvement in self-efficacy translates into other areas of life, making it easier to cope with emotional challenges.

Self-efficacy, a concept introduced by psychologist Albert Bandura, refers to an individual's belief in their ability to succeed in specific situations or accomplish a task. High self-efficacy enhances one's resilience to stress, as it promotes a proactive rather than reactive approach to life's challenges. People who believe in their ability to influence their own well-being are more likely to engage in health-promoting behaviours, such as regular exercise, mindful movement, and stress management techniques. Conversely, individuals with low self-efficacy may feel helpless in the face of stress and are less likely to take positive action. Movement, particularly when practiced regularly and with intention, can significantly boost self-efficacy by demonstrating to individuals that they have control over their bodies and, by extension, their emotional well-being. Furthermore, engaging in movement with others—whether through team sports, group fitness classes, or community-based activities—adds a social dimension that enhances resilience. Social support is a critical factor in stress management and emotional resilience. When individuals move together, they not only benefit from the physical act of movement but also from the shared experience, which can create feelings of belonging, reduce loneliness, and provide a support network during challenging times. This sense of community, reinforced through movement, helps buffer the negative effects of stress and enhances emotional well-being.

Movement as preventive care: long-term benefits for stress management

One of the most profound benefits of integrating movement into daily life is its role in preventive care. Movement not only helps alleviate immediate symptoms of stress but also strengthens the body and mind to handle future stressors more effectively. Regular physical activity contributes to long-term stress management by enhancing cardiovascular health, improving sleep quality, and promoting emotional regulation—all key factors in building resilience to stress. Long-term physical activity has been shown to reduce the risk of developing chronic stress-related conditions such as hypertension, heart disease, and diabetes. By maintaining a healthy level of physical fitness, individuals can reduce the physical toll that stress takes on the body. Aerobic exercises like running, swimming, and cycling are known to improve cardiovascular health, which is closely tied to stress management. The British Heart Association recommends at least 150 minutes of moderate-intensity aerobic activity per week for optimal heart health, which also serves to reduce stress and improve overall well-being.

Additionally, movement positively impacts sleep quality—a crucial factor in stress resilience. Poor sleep is both a symptom and a cause of stress, creating a vicious cycle where stress disrupts sleep, and lack of sleep exacerbates stress. Regular exercise, particularly when done earlier in the day, helps regulate the sleep-wake cycle (circadian rhythm) and promotes deeper, more restorative sleep. In turn, better sleep enhances emotional regulation, concentration, and energy levels, making it easier to cope with daily stressors. Moreover, movement fosters long-term emotional regulation by promoting mindfulness and self-awareness. Many movement practices, such as yoga, tai chi, and mindful walking, encourage individuals to focus on the present moment and tune into their bodily sensations. This mindfulness not only helps alleviate immediate stress but also builds long-term emotional resilience by teaching individuals to respond to stressors with greater awareness and less reactivity. In the long run, individuals who regularly engage in mindful movement develop a greater capacity for emotional regulation, which serves as a buffer against the chronic effects of stress.

SMALL MOVEMENTS, BIG IMPACT: GETTING STARTED WITH PHYSICAL ACTIVITY

For many, the idea of engaging in physical movement as a response to stress can seem overwhelming, especially if they feel demotivated or mentally exhausted. This is common in people experiencing high stress levels, anxiety, or depression, where the body's natural inclination is to retreat and conserve energy. Yet, it is precisely in these moments that small acts of movement can have the greatest impact.

Physical activity does not always mean an intense workout. Even simple movements, such as stretching, walking, or practicing deep breathing exercises, can significantly alter our emotional state. For example, stretching while waiting for the kettle to boil, or doing a brief body scan in the morning, allows us to incorporate small, achievable shifts in our daily routine. These small steps can make the larger task of engaging in regular exercise feel more manageable and less intimidating. Moreover, movement as a strategy for coping with stress does not have to follow a rigid structure. Micro-movements, such as pacing while talking on the phone or doing household chores with greater mindfulness, can also activate the nervous system in a positive way. Incorporating these brief periods of physical engagement throughout the day can break up long stretches of inactivity and mitigate the buildup of tension in the body.

Motivation often builds through small, incremental changes. Just as we might take a gradual approach to therapy or learning a new skill, physical movement requires patience and experimentation. You may not immediately enjoy every Pilates or yoga class, but just like counselling, it is a process of trial, error, and repetition. Exploring different types of activities, teachers, and classes so that you find something you enjoy is essential to building a sustainable relationship with movement.

Incorporating movement into daily life: practical strategies for stress relief

For many people, the idea of incorporating regular movement into an already busy, stress-filled life may seem daunting. However, movement doesn't need to be confined to structured exercise sessions at the gym. There are many simple, accessible ways to integrate movement into daily routines that can help manage stress without feeling overwhelming. These strategies are particularly helpful for individuals who may feel too stressed or exhausted to engage in formal exercise but still want to experience the benefits of physical activity.

1. **Desk stretches**: Many people spend long hours sitting at a desk, which can contribute to physical tension and mental fatigue. Incorporating short stretching sessions throughout the workday can alleviate this tension and provide a mental reset. Simple neck rolls, shoulder shrugs, and seated spinal twists can help reduce stress and improve focus.

2. **Walking breaks**: Taking a short walk, even for just 10 to 15 minutes, can significantly reduce stress levels and improve mood. Walking outdoors, particularly in nature, has the added benefit of exposure to natural light and fresh air, which can enhance the mood-boosting effects of movement. These mini breaks also provide a moment of mindfulness, allowing individuals to step away from their stressors and reset their mental state.

3. **Mindful movement practices**: Mindfulness does not always require stillness. Practices like mindful walking or mindful stretching combine movement with focused attention on the body, breath, and surroundings. These activities help ground individuals in the present moment, reducing the tendency to ruminate on stressors and promoting a sense of calm.

4. **Movement while multitasking**: For those with particularly hectic schedules, finding ways to incorporate movement into daily tasks can be a simple but effective strategy. For example, doing calf raises while brushing your teeth, squatting while folding laundry, or stretching while watching TV are all ways to add movement to routine activities. These small acts of movement may seem insignificant but can accumulate over time, contributing to better stress management and overall well-being.

5. **Evening stretching routine**: Many people find it difficult to wind down at the end of a stressful day, which can impact sleep quality. A simple evening stretching routine, focusing on slow, deliberate movements and deep breathing, can help release physical tension and signal to the body that it's time to relax. This practice not only improves flexibility and reduces muscle tightness but also enhances sleep quality, making it easier to face the next day's stressors with a calm and focused mind.

Movement as a tool for managing stress

In conclusion, movement is an essential tool for managing stress, offering benefits that span the physical, mental, and emotional spectrum. Whether through aerobic exercise, yoga, Pilates, or simple stretching, movement helps regulate the brain's chemistry, reduce physical tension, and foster emotional resilience. By integrating both eastern philosophies and modern scientific understandings of how movement affects the brain and body, we can develop a more holistic approach to stress management. Movement allows us to reconnect with our bodies, process emotions, and build the confidence needed to face life's challenges head-on. Moreover, movement is not just a reactive strategy for dealing with stress; it is also a powerful preventive measure. Regular physical activity strengthens the body and mind, enhances emotional regulation, and fosters long-term resilience to stress. By making movement a daily practice, individuals can protect themselves from the harmful effects of chronic stress and enjoy a more balanced, fulfilling life. Whether it's taking a walk in nature, practicing yoga, or dancing to your favourite song, movement offers a simple yet profoundly effective way to manage stress and enhance well-being. By embracing movement as a key component of stress management, we can empower ourselves to lead healthier, more resilient lives.

5

TYPES OF STRESS AND DEBUNKING THE COMMON MYTHS

Stress often makes a daily appearance and features frequently within our thoughts and conversations. In this chapter we explore how stress is a double-edged sword, as some of it is necessary, managing this daily stress can help you make it a superpower to help you perform. However, when it tips over the threshold, it can become a deterrent which affects our overall wellbeing. Stress moves from acute to chronic, we will explore can strategies that prevent us from getting into the chronic phase. We explore how the taboos associate with both the mental and physical aspects and bring together a more wholistic but well evidenced perspective.

MOVING FROM ACUTE TO CHRONIC STRESS

Acute refers to immediate, while chronic is more a long-term experience in the sense of experiencing stress. Very often one experiences stress due to an event in the present. This could be an interview, assessment, change in life circumstances, pregnancy, a new diagnosis or sudden change in life. However, if the individual is more aware and able to manage stress and/or is aware of triggers and can

DOI: 10.4324/9781003537410-5

deal with the stress, they may be able to overcome this acute stress. Recently, there is more evidence suggesting that the long-term consequences of acute stress may provide more critical information to understanding the role of stress in psychological disorders (Musazzi et al., 2017).

Chronic stress is often the stress than has built up in the individual over time. Specifically, initially the stress would have been caused by a one-off event, but keeping in mind the risk factors, individual differences and other factors, the stress builds up and over time the individual may experience stress across different domains. Built up of chronic stress could happen either consciously or even unconsciously in some cases. If an individual is not aware of one's own response or is not reflecting on their life or life changes – they may notice how stress develops. But notice it only when it affects the person's life drastically. In some cases when an individual experiences an acute stress and due to various reason, may not be able to deal with this effectively – they may get stuck in a cycle of being stressed. Which over times, gets overwhelming for the individual, then the person avoids situations that may cause stress, rather than finding effective coping strategies.

HOW IS PHYSICAL AND MENTAL HEALTH LINKED TO STRESS AND COPING?

Within psychology a framework often commonly discussed is the bio-psycho-social model. In this model, stress in the individual's life is not discounted but is integrated to the experience of their physical and/or mental health. Within a lot of recent formulations, stress is commonly thought of to be one of the risk factors to developing certain conditions (physical and/or mental health related). So, depending on how the individual copes with associated stress, if they are unable to manage it over time, it may make the individual vulnerable to other physical and mental health issues. There is more evidence regarding the impact of stress on mental and physical health today.

Stress is known to (e.g. Cohen, 2000; MacLeod, 2023) have a negative impact over time both on one's mental and physical health. Hence, it's important for us to understand our own stressors and triggers. Having a better understanding, allows the individual to also find a strategy or coping methods that can help overcome the stress. Finally, it is important to be aware of our own bias and/or the role of stigma around accessing well-being resources. Given that we are more a global community, there is a role of culture that plays an important role in the way one perceives stress and goes to a default coping strategy. There are a lot of common strategies people use to cope with stress, especially when it may be a one of event. However, when it becomes more chronic and has led to changes in one's physical, mental and health domains, it become crucial for the individual to be able to seek support either from relevant trained medical and/or support health workers to create an individualised plan.

Common strategies to cope with stress could vary across physical, breathwork and/or cognitive strategies like planning-organising. Coping strategies can be both positive and negative. Sometimes, negative strategies may work briefly, but if the "go to" is always negative – it may not withstand the test of time. When we are faced with stress, most often procrastination is something we all do.– In certain small aspects or with conscious procrastination, it can be good, but if it goes towards avoidance of life or work, then the scale is tipping towards a negative coping style. When we procrastinate, we come up with cleaning activities, to-do lists, watch movies, speak to friends etc. So, we not only procrastinate – to avoid that stressful activity, but use other activities that soothe our nerves and allow us to cope temporarily. Stress in some individuals often allows them to explore physical activities like going out, using the gym, working out, meeting friends, swimming, dancing etc. This again is important to take the mind of the anxiety and using physical methods to calm our-selves down to eventually deal with the stress. Similarly using cognitive strategies like planning, organising, thinking changing jobs, aligning to our inner calling are more cognitive or self-reflective approaches to dealing with stress.

THE COMMON MYTHS AROUND STRESS

"Stress" is a word used very often when people describe the sense of feeling overwhelmed. We often do not necessarily link it to a physical or mental status. Stress levels also play an important role in manage our ability to cope with distress in everyday life. Certain myths around stress are very common, in the following section we aim to discuss some of these and debunk the myths or taboos.

If you do not have symptoms, you do not have stress. When an individual says they may be stressed, people often may say you really do not have any symptoms, so how can you have stress? In passing such a quite vague comment and questioning the person's experience, we are not only not acknowledging their experience but also suggesting that you need to have symptoms to experience stress. The symptoms of stress vary across individuals and not everyone may experience identical symptoms.

If you are busy, it means that you are stressed. The common assumption is that if you are busy and have a tight schedule, you may be stressed. That's not always true. Yes, certain type of people like this and how stressful situations may affect them may vary – but just because you are busy does not imply you are stressed. There may be people who do like to have a busy lifestyle and not be stressed. One of the authors (SF) is someone who likes to engage in several activities. She often does engage with multitasking, which some people may find very stressful. As she was trying to conceive and work towards having a child, several people told her, stop being stressed – don't do so much. However, her gynaecologist who knew her advised her not to worry – just carry on doing what you do. But you know your body, if you feel tired or stressed or burnt out – reduce what you are doing. Just being busy does not mean you are stressed! So, SF had to explain this to friends who kept telling her she was stressed, when she was not. However, if SF had to change her way of life – it would have been more stressful for her. Stress can often have emotional, behavioural, cognitive, and/or physical symptoms. Very often even the symptoms across these domains would vary considerably.

Stress is same for everyone. Not all of us experience stress in the same way and not every activity is equally stressful. There are number of factors that contributes to the experience of stress. This would include the individual's early childhood experiences, the individual's resilience, experiences, current life situations, financial stability etc. Some individuals may thrive when in pressure and for someone else, this might be a source of excessive stress. Some people love to drive and may not cause any stress while there may be others, who find that driving can be very stressful.

Stress is always bad for us. Again, we assume stress is bad. However, a little bit of stress can allow one to be more motivated and helps keep the balance in life. But like everything else, too much of it can tip the scale and cause us to feel overwhelmed and we may not manage it well anymore. Not having any stress can make us feel demotivated and not recognise a larger sense of meaning to life. Having some stress, like having some anxiety is needed to keep us going and to keep check on our sense of self and worth.

Alcohol helps reduce stress. Often in a social setting, we look at social drinking or alcohol as a self-help strategy. But sometimes we assume drinking or drugs help manage stress. However, when our body systems are stressed, using alcohol or drugs, may give us some initial numbness to deal with stress but not be an ideal long-term strategy. In addition, if the individual does get addicted to alcohol or drugs, it may become a more default coping mechanism or avoidance of the stress but may not really allow the individual to find more useful or different strategies.

Most popular stress management strategies are the best. Often stress is a common topic in popular magazines. Very often we hear about coaches, psychologists or counsellors talking about the current effective stress management techniques such as cold-water therapy, mindfulness and spending time outside. Whilst these are often helpful it is necessary to comprehensively identify your own stress or stressors and work on the unique strategies that may work effectively for you. Often relying on self-help books and/or blogs may not be the best way to deal with your stress. Even though they may seem intriguing, we need to be aware that individualised coping strategies are always more effective and sustainable over time.

You can ignore minor stress and worry about paying attention to only major stress. Many times when you notice stress in your life, it's normally minor. But as always if you do not nip it in the bud, it would be more difficult to manage it when it gets out of hand. Having strategies that are effective will always help and if you can manage minor stressors, you are more prepared when you encounter a more major stress symptom. Often when you do not pay attention to the minor stress levels and wait till it becomes a major issue and have symptoms (physical or mental) you may have to work much harder to make larger and more long-term life changes.

Only one or two strategies work to manage stress. Stress can be managed using more than one method. For some people a good bath may work help manage stress, but for some sitting in a bath can itself be stressful especially with constant disruptions, say for example she may have young kids and may be worrying about what's happening in the other room. Some individuals may cope better with a busier schedule, while others may prefer to share their experience over a cuppa with a friend. Someone might prefer to use talking therapies or access psychotherapy sessions, while others may find running, Pilates or yoga as a great method to manage their stress. So, it's not just one approach but a combination of options may work or suit you best. It is important to also remember to be flexible, as some methods may work better than others, depending on the cause or symptom of stress.

You can avoid stress. Wrong, stress cannot be avoided. Stress may come from different facets of life. Sometimes individuals may be very resilient and hence may have a better way to deal automatically with everyday stressors they may not even notice. But if they experience any adverse events like, loss of work, a break-up or separation, or death of a loved one, they may suddenly find it difficult to cope. This may then bring on thoughts like, "*this cannot happen to me,*" or "*I cannot deal with this, I am not good enough*" etc. So, we may not be able to avoid stress, but some people manage it better or more automatically. Therefore, it is important for us to recognise the triggers and find effective ways to manage this stress.

Stress cannot cause medical problems. As mentioned, this is untrue, the fact is that stress can cause physical, medical and/or health problems linked with mental health and wellbeing. Often also referred to as functional disorders or psychosomatic disorders the root cause of these can be stress, which had not been identified and managed at an early stage. Very often the person's personality or ability to manage stress can directly manifest into more physical or medical symptoms, therefore indirectly being manifested in a different form. However, such experiences would need to be addressed from different perspectives at times, so you may need to investigate a more multi-team approach. Here, with medical professionals, you can deal with some symptoms, by using more physical approaches like exercise, or mediation to change or improve coping or grounding skills while also exploring counselling or therapy to deal with more long-term coping strategies.

The above myths are what are very common and have been discussed with the intention to understand these from a factual perspective. However, often the term "stress" is casually used in passing, but it is important to also understand the difference between acute and chronic stress.

6

ROAD LESS TRAVELLED

In this chapter we integrate the evidence from both practical and scientific aspects. We continue to support how the reader can become more knowledgeable in their mind and body while recognising their own triggers and stress responses. Especially, as stress, while being deeply personal, is also a universal experience. The techniques and methods can not only be useful for people interested in stress. Integrating scientific and clinical practices, this chapter offers actionable strategies and reflections, guiding readers to carve their unique path in managing stress.

THE MIND-BODY CONNECTION: A COMPASS FOR COPING

Understanding the intricate relationship between the mind and body is fundamental to navigating stress effectively. The physical sensations associated with stress such as tight muscles, a racing heart, or shallow breathing, are not isolated occurrences, but are deeply intertwined with our mental and emotional states. Recognising this interplay can transform our understanding of stress from a purely external challenge into an internal dialogue. By tuning into the body's signals, we can identify stress triggers more effectively and develop strategies to manage our responses. This mind-body connection acts as a compass, guiding us towards balance and well-being. Often this

DOI: 10.4324/9781003537410-6

aspect is neglected, and we tend to focus on common practices to cope with stress.

One powerful way to enhance this connection is through the practice of body scanning. This involves setting aside a few quiet moments each day to mentally scan your body from head to toe. With your eyes closed, direct your attention to each part of your body in turn, noticing areas of tension or discomfort. Once identified, consciously relax these areas, releasing any built-up stress and tension. This practice will ground you in the present and heighten your awareness of how stress can manifest physically before it escalates. It is important to start integrating these practices on a regular basis, so that when faced with a trigger or stress, this can be easily accessible and something that you are familiar with. In terms of managing stress, we commonly address it only when we experience stress, in fact it is important to build in more regular practices and coping strategies in your everyday life.

Breathing awareness is another technique which uses the natural rhythm of the breath to regulate the stress response. The breath acts as a bridge between the body and mind, with its patterns often mirroring our emotional states. For instance, shallow, rapid breaths can signal heightened anxiety. By practicing controlled breathing techniques, such as diaphragmatic breathing or alternate nostril breathing, we can engage the parasympathetic nervous system which will relax the body's response (see Chapter 2 for more details). This helps to slow the heart rate, lower blood pressure, and instil a sense of calm. These simple practices offer immediate relief and create a habit of mindfulness that supports long-term resilience.

Movement is another invaluable tool for fostering the mind-body connection. Activities such as yoga, Pilates, or even a mindful walk can help relax and de-stress you. These practices encourage physical release while fostering a meditative state, harmonising body and mind. Pilates and yoga combine physical postures with breath control and mindfulness, creating a physical response that reduces cortisol levels and enhances emotional regulation. Similarly, tai chi's flowing movements promotes inner calm, while walking mindfully in nature can provide clarity and a sense of perspective. These movement-based practices not only alleviate physical tension but also support neurological pathways that promote stress resilience.

By cultivating this connection between the mind and body, you can gain a clearer understanding of your stress responses, this self-awareness becomes the foundation for personalised coping strategies. Through consistent practice, these techniques can transform stress from a disruptive force into a manageable aspect of life, empowering individuals to navigate challenges with greater ease and balance. It is only recently there is more evidence in bringing together the usual coping strategies with more holistic approaches, which is a new but very encouraging additional road to learning to cope with stress. Professionals can utilise this progress to widen their interventions and support for individuals incorporating traditional support with holistic practices.

INTEGRATING STRESS REDUCING PRACTICES INTO EVERYDAY LIFE

Therapeutic strategies need not be confined to formal clinical set-tings. They can be woven seamlessly into the fabric of everyday life, offering small but significant ways to manage stress. By integrat-ing these techniques into daily routines, individuals can cultivate a sense of control and resilience without requiring extensive time or resources. These approaches provide a practical framework for reduc-ing stress and enhancing well-being.

One of the most transformative everyday therapeutic strate-gies is the power of pausing. In the relentless pace of modern life, stress often arises from the pressure to keep moving, accomplish-ing, and responding without respite. We all feel obliged to quickly respond to text messages or emails. Pausing creates a moment of intentional stillness, allowing the mind and body to recalibrate. It could be as simple as taking a few deep breaths during a stressful meeting, savouring the taste and aroma of your morning coffee without the distraction of screens, or stepping outside to feel the sun on your skin for a moment. These intentional pauses disrupt the cycle of stress, grounding you in the present and restoring a sense of calm.

Gratitude practices are another accessible tool for everyday stress management. The simple act of focusing on what you appreciate can have profound effects on your mental health. Research has shown that by regularly practicing gratitude you can shift attention away from stressors towards sources of joy, fostering a more positive outlook. Spending a few minutes each evening jotting down three things you are grateful for, whether it is a kind gesture from a friend, a moment of laughter, or the beauty of a sunset, you can reframe your day and cultivate a habit of mindfulness. This practice nurtures an optimistic mindset, reducing the emotional weight of daily stress.

Visualisation and reframing offer a creative and empowering way to interact with stress. Visualising stress as a wave, a natural, temporary phenomenon that rises, peaks, and eventually recedes, can provide a sense of perspective and control. This imagery helps remind you that stress is not a permanent state but a transient experience. Pairing this visualisation with reframing techniques, such as identifying potential opportunities for growth or learning within a challenging situation, can further transform how stress is perceived. Instead of viewing stress as a threat, you begin to see it as something manageable, and even meaningful.

These strategies demonstrate that therapeutic principles don't need to be complex or time consuming to be effective. By embedding these practices into your everyday routine, you create a toolkit for managing stress that is both accessible and adaptable. Over time, these small, meaningful actions accumulate, fostering a resilient mindset that empowers you to navigate life's challenges with greater ease and confidence.

SUPPORTING OTHERS THROUGH STRESS

Supporting someone through stress is an act of compassion and empathy that can significantly alleviate their burden. Stress often feels isolating, leaving individuals overwhelmed and disconnected. As a family member or friend, your presence and understanding can serve as a powerful buffer against the challenges they face. By cultivating thoughtful and empathetic support, you not only help them navigate their stress but also strengthen the bond you share.

One of the most meaningful ways to support someone experiencing stress is through active listening. When people feel heard, they often experience a profound sense of relief and connection. This means giving them your full attention without interrupting or immediately offering solutions. Instead of trying to "fix" the problem, let them express their thoughts and emotions freely. Ideally, avoiding making judgmental comments or gestures. Your role as a listener is not to provide answers but to create a safe space where they feel understood. This simple act of being present can often be more powerful than any advice you might give.

Validating their experience is equally important. Stress can feel minimised or dismissed when met with phrases like "just relax" or "it's not that bad." Such responses, even if well-intentioned, can deepen feelings of frustration or isolation. Instead, acknowledge their feelings with empathy. A statement like, "that sounds incredibly overwhelming. I'm here for you," conveys understanding and support. Validation does not require you to agree with their perspective, it simply shows that you respect their emotions and recognise the weight of their challenges.

Offering practical help can make a tangible difference for someone under stress. When stress takes over, even routine tasks can feel insurmountable. Small acts of assistance like running an errand, preparing a meal, or offering childcare, can ease their load and create space for them to breathe. Be specific in your offers to help, instead of saying, "Let me know if you need anything," try, "I'm free this weekend, can I help with groceries or errands?" These gestures show initiative and make your support more actionable.

Respecting boundaries is another essential aspect of supporting others. While it's natural to want to help, remember that each person's relationship with stress is unique. Some may welcome close involvement, while others need space to process their emotions independently. Encourage them to seek professional support if their stress feels unmanageable but avoid pushing them into actions that they are not ready for. Respect their pace and choices, ensuring that your efforts align with their comfort level. By approaching stressed loved ones with empathy, active listening, practical assistance, and respect, you create a foundation of support that empowers their resilience. Your role is not to solve their stress but to walk alongside them, offering kindness and understanding as they find their way through. In doing so, you not only help them cope but also deepen the trust and connection within your relationship.

BRINGING TOGETHER THE KEY CONCEPTS FROM THE CHAPTERS

We started the book by emphasising the importance of context and illustrating how stress can be either a constructive force or a precursor to anxiety and other issues. The idea was to challenge the reader to remain curious about their own stress thresholds and introduced the framework for understanding how different life events, daily pressures, and individual perceptions shape stress responses. We then we briefly gave an overview of the physiological underpinnings of stress, revealing how the autonomic nervous system orchestrates our responses. Understanding the roles of the sympathetic and parasympathetic nervous system, the second chapter illuminated how stress can be manifested in our body and its potential

to contribute to physical and mental health issues when left unnoticed. We briefly introduced coping mechanisms rooted in biological awareness, underscoring the importance of proactive strategies to manage the impact of stress on health and well-being. While the third chapter went beyond the physiology to understand the role of cultural, ethnic and neurodiverse perspectives into dealing with stress. It explored the challenges faced by neurodivergent individuals, emphasising how neurodiversity intersects with stress in unique ways. Additionally, the chapter integrated some cultural and historical perspectives of stress. The fourth chapter turned to the power of physical activity as a tool for stress recovery. This chapter also spotlighted the therapeutic benefits of certain practices with roots in eastern philosophies like yoga, Pilates, and tai chi. By addressing the somatic responses to stress and unresolved trauma, the chapter presented movement as a gateway to emotional healing and resilience, furthering the mind-body connection established in earlier chapters. The next chapter further explores the myths or misconceptions surrounding stress. By exploring strategies to help prevent the escalation from acute to chronic stress, offering evidence-based insights to shift societal attitudes and to empower individuals to see stress as both a challenge and an opportunity for growth. In the last chapter we integrate these lessons into actionable insights. This chapter emphasises the importance of recognising personal triggers and responses, encouraging readers to cultivate self-awareness as a pathway to resilience. Practical techniques for navigating stress, grounded in therapeutic and everyday approaches, are presented alongside guidance on supporting others. The mind-body connection, brain-based strategies, and movement-based therapies discussed in earlier chapters converge here, forming a cohesive blueprint for managing stress holistically.

We hope as you navigated through this book, you may have not only gained a deeper understanding of stress but also a range of tools to approach your own stress thoughtfully, whether for personal growth or professional application. The road less travelled is one of curiosity, reflection, and empowerment, an invitation to transform stress from a source of struggle into a catalyst for strength and self-discovery. This book is not merely a guide but an invitation to venture into the uncharted paths of your relationship with stress, especially as you know your body and mind better than anyone else. Experts, counsellors and psychologists are here to support you, but the catalyst for the change lies within your own self and awareness. Taking an unfamiliar journey often requires more than just an intellectual understanding, it calls for curiosity, courage, and a commitment to self-discovery. Moments when you may struggle, are not failures but part of the process, a reminder to return to your practices, draw on your strengths, and seek support when needed. Above all, the road less travelled is about forging a path that feels authentic to you. It honours your individuality and respects that no single strategy or philosophy works for everyone. It is about stepping away from well-known strategies and conventional narratives about stress to uncover what truly resonates with you as an individual. This journey may not be straightforward, but it promises transformation, growth, and an enriched connection to yourself and others.

REFERENCES

American Psychological Association. (2015). Stress. In *APA dictionary of psychology* (2nd ed.).

Bartholomew, J. B., Stults-Kolehmainen, M. A., Elrod, C. C., & Todd, J. S. (2008). Strength gains after resistance training: The effect of stressful, negative life events. *The Journal of Strength & Conditioning Research*, 22(4), 1215–1221.

Bratman, G. N., Daily, G. C., Levy, B. J., & Gross, J. J. (2015). The benefits of nature experience: Improved affect and cognition. *Landscape and Urban Planning*, 138, 41–50.

Cannon, W. B. (1914) The emergency function of the adrenal medulla in pain and the major emotions. *American Journal Physiology*, 33, 356–372.

Chekroud, S. R., Gueorguieva, R., Zheutlin, A. B., Paulus, M., Krumholz, H. M., Krystal, J. H., & Chekroud, A. M. (2018). Association between physical exercise and mental health in 1·2 million individuals in the USA between 2011 and 2015: a cross-sectional study. *The Lancet Psychiatry*, 5(9), 739–746.

Cohen, J. I. (2000). Stress and mental health: a biobehavioral perspective. *Issues in Mental Health Nursing*, 21(2), 185–202. https://doi.org/10.1080/01612840 0248185

Cotman, C. W., & Berchtold, N. C. (2002). Exercise: a behavioral intervention to enhance brain health and plasticity. *Trends in Neurosciences*, 25(6), 295–301.

Eberth, J., & Sedlmeier, P. (2012). The effects of mindfulness meditation: A meta-analysis. *Mindfulness*, 3(3), 174–189.

Hamer, M., Taylor, A., & Steptoe, A. (2006). The effect of acute aerobic exercise on stress related blood pressure responses: A systematic review and meta-analysis. *Biological Psychology*, 71(2), 183–190.

Hopper, S. I., Murray, S. L., Ferrara, L. R., & Singleton, J. K. (2019). Effectiveness of diaphragmatic breathing for reducing physiological and psychological stress in adults: A quantitative systematic review. *JBI Evidence Synthesis, 17*(9), 1855–1876.

Hutson, P., & Hutson, J. (2024). Enhancing flow states in neurodivergent individuals through cognitive network integration. *Global Health Economics and Sustainability, 4345.* https://accscience.com/journal/GHES/0/0/10.36922/ghes.4345

Kabat-Zinn, J. (2003). *Mindfulness-based interventions in context: Past, present, and future.* Springer.

Kabat-Zinn, J. (2015). Mindfulness. *Mindfulness, 6*(6), 1481–1483.

Kwak, S., Lee, T. Y., Jung, W. H., Hur, J. W., Bae, D., Hwang, W. J., . . . & Kwon, J. S. (2019). The immediate and sustained positive effects of meditation on resilience are mediated by changes in the resting brain. *Frontiers in Human Neuroscience, 13,* 436625.

Leung, M. K., Lau, W. K., Chan, C. C., Wong, S. S., Fung, A. L., & Lee, T. M. (2018). Meditation-induced neuroplastic changes in amygdala activity during negative affective processing. *Social Neuroscience, 13*(3), 277–288.

MacLeod, K. J., English, S., Ruuskanen, S. K., & Taborsky, B. (2023). Stress in the social context: A behavioural and eco-evolutionary perspective. *Journal of Experimental Biology, 226*(15).

Marten, W. D., & Wilkerson, B. (2003). Stress, work and mental health: A global perspective. *Acta Neuropsychiatrica, 15*(1), 44–53.

McGonigal, K. (2019). *The joy of movement: How exercise helps us find happiness, hope, connection, and courage.* Penguin.

Musazzi, L., Tornese, P., Sala, N., & Popoli, M. (2017). Acute or chronic? A stressful question. *Trends in Neurosciences, 40*(9), 525–535.

Porges, S. W. (2011). *The polyvagal theory: Neurophysiological foundations of emotions, attachment, communication, and self-regulation* (Norton series on interpersonal neurobiology). WW Norton & Company.

Rowland, D. (2024). *Decoding Neurophysiological Differences in the Autistic Brain.* https://scholar.google.com/scholar?hl=en&as_sdt=0%2C5&q=Rowland%2C+D.+%282024%29.+Decoding+Neurophysiological+Differences+in+the+Autistic+Brain&btnG=

Ströhle, A. (2009). Physical activity, exercise, depression and anxiety disorders. *Journal of Neural Transmission, 116,* 777–784.

Tsutsumi, T., Don, B. M., Zaichkowsky, L. D., Takenaka, K., Oka, K., & Ohno, T. (1998). Comparison of high and moderate intensity of strength training on mood and anxiety in older adults. *Perceptual and Motor Skills*, 87(3), 1003–1011.

Van der Kolk, Bessel A (2014). The body keeps the score: Brain, mind, and body in the healing of trauma. Viking.

Ye, Y., Lin, H., Wan, M., Qiu, P., Xia, R., He, J., . . . & Zheng, G. (2021). The effects of aerobic exercise on oxidative stress in older adults: A systematic review and meta-analysis. *Frontiers in Physiology*, 12, 701151.

Yerkes, R. M., & Dodson, J. D. (1908). The relation of strength of stimulus to rapidity of habit-formation. *Journal of Comparative Neurology and Psychology*, 18(5), 459–482.